CW00865026

ISBN 13: 978-1979440783

ISBN-10: 1 9794 4078 6

Marketing Teacher Ltd, Chichester, United Kingdom, PO19 3QP

First published 2017.

www.marketingteacher.com

To Petra and Jack.

Table of contents

Chapter 1 Marketing for you.

This is where YOU start marketing.

Why *you*? When *you* become an entrepreneur, start-up or small business, it starts with *you*, it is all about *you*, and without *you* it will not happen.

Whilst this fact may seem obvious, this view of the world of marketing runs contrary to popular thinking. Marketing should be about your customers; your main goal as a business person is to meet the requirements of customers, which will ultimately mean that you make profits which eventually lead to a successful enterprise. Yes – of course this is true, but it is only part of *your story*.

When you embark on the road to entrepreneurship, and start your own business, it is seldom only to make huge bags of cash. The step, whether you made it some time ago or you intend to make it tomorrow, is unlikely to have been entirely with the aim of becoming a billionaire (although do not disregard this thought for now). People market ideas, products and services for all sorts of reasons; you might want to make the world better for everyone, you might desire recognition for yourself, you might not like working for other people, or you might have found yourself unemployed for a whole range of reasons. That is why you have arrived here, and now you need to develop your marketing knowledge and skills.

This book is written for *you*.

Having worked for others and for myself, I have built a whole range of practical marketing skills that you can use today. I have also taught the academic tools, models and concepts of marketing to university students for 20 years, and I have written and delivered marketing training for dozens of entrepreneurs, start-ups and small businesses. From my experiences, I have learned important lessons about marketing, which are shared with you throughout this book.

Some might say that marketing is academic and only highly intelligent people know the truth about marketing. No, this is not true. Others might say that marketing is practical, and only people that 'do' marketing know the truth about marketing. Again, this is not true.

Marketing is about you, and this book will deliver marketing thinking and practice in easily understood sections so that you can start marketing today. It blends the best from marketing academia and practical marketing to give you the best approaches, hints and tips.

You and your marketing skills.

Your book is built in a series of sections. The first half of the book is about traditional, offline marketing tools and techniques, and the second half of this book is about digital marketing approaches. It anticipates that you know nothing or little about marketing, and then will take you to a point where you can confidently market your idea, start-up or small business. The book contains audit sheets to help you condense new learning into half a page of notes, or even less. What will you learn about marketing?

The book begins with you. As a person, you will already have a series of marketing opportunities at your fingertips, that you can use to kick-start your idea, start-up, or small business. Despite what you may think, you already have some skills, experience and resources. Think about what you might want to gain from marketing, but also consider what might be an affordable loss as you get underway. You will recognise, respond to and reshape opportunities as you build your business, so be flexible. It is about *You and marketing*.

You need to *Know your customers*. You will find out the 15 most important questions to ask about your customers. Where will you find your customers? 8 key ways to gather new information are explained, and 15 ways to take advantage of current information are described. You will also discover 20 fundamental tips to make your networking more effective.

You will begin by forming *Your marketing mix*. The marketing mix is a fundamental toolkit which is used to make your day-to-day marketing a success. You will learn how you use the marketing mix to control pricing, products/services, promotion, distribution, people, marketing processes, and the physical attributes of marketing - from website look and feel, to premises look and feel. Core chapters of this book look at parts of the marketing mix in greater detail, and in a practical and useful way.

You will need to **Get your price right**. Pricing sounds simple, but is likely to be one of the most confusing and tricky tasks for any small business. Let us look at a menu of different tools and techniques that you can use to make sure that you charge the right price, for the right product or service, at the right time, for the right customers. So why is pricing so tricky? Why do so many small business owners scratch their heads when it comes to placing a figure on a product or service? It is all about getting your price right!

As you begin your journey to success, you will need to start selling. This is likely to mean that you will go face-to-face with customers, and you will sell yourself. This means that you will be responsible for selling, at least in the early days, and that you need to market yourself as part of the idea, product or service that you are marketing. There are chapters on *Sell yourself* and *Promoting yourself*. Promoting yourself covers a multitude of practical tools and approaches to make sure that you communicate effectively with the outside world. These sections cover everything that you need from cheap, do-it-yourself advertising, to a full campaign using an advertising agency.

Sections on promotion develop into more detailed, practical advice on Public Relations (Public relations for you) and blogging (Writing a successful blog). Public Relations is simply how you communicate with your public and with the media. As you launch or grow your business, you will depend upon your reputation for survival and success. If you are new to blogging, then the whole topic of writing a successful blog for your small business, idea or start-up, may seem a little daunting. The book will consider the pros and cons of a blog, and offer advice and tips on how to make your blog more compelling.

How about *Organising an event* to promote your business? When organising an event, you will need a process which will make your endeavour a success. By using a simple Five Ws and How approach you give yourself an overview – Who? What? When? Where? Why? and How?

The second half of this book is to get you up and running with your digital marketing. The initial advice will *Get you started with digital marketing*. Digital marketing is ever-changing. If you are part of the generation of people who has grown up with technology, you will undoubtedly find the challenges of digital marketing exciting and stimulating; if you have not, then the anticipation of embarking upon digital marketing will possibly be more daunting. Either way, these chapters will offer practical advice on how to tackle your digital marketing.

How will you approach *Your websites and online stores*? You will need to decide whether you build your own website or whether you pay for the services of a professional developer. Will you need an online store(s)? Or perhaps Amazon or eBay are more suitable for getting your products to market. Perhaps you will decide that advertising online is the best way to employ your digital marketing efforts. On the other hand, your digital marketing activities might focus on communication, and therefore, e-mail marketing will be important to your company. Whether you are a manufacturer, a distributor, professional or service provider, your website will need some *Search Engine Optimisation (SEO)* and we demystify SEO and offer some simple tips to help your website rank as highly as possible in the search engines.

Your social media will undoubtedly be a very important part of your digital marketing strategy for your small business. You may be an expert or you may need to seek some assistance. If you use social media yourself, then you are more likely to find social media marketing straightforward. However, as is often the case, some individuals simply prefer to retain their privacy and do not participate in any kind of social media activities. It is probable that you will be one or the other of these two types of person. Your book will take your through social media marketing, step-by-step, with plenty of hints and tips.

For your start-up or small business, it is likely that your customers will like to hear from you again. *Your e-mail marketing* is an ideal medium for you to stay in regular touch with your customers. As with much digital marketing for small businesses, you can make this as simple or complex as you like. You can set-up and run your email marketing with guidance and advice from this chapter.

How do you know that you are on the right marketing track, or that you have achieved success? By *Measuring your marketing success*, you will be able to use largely FREE online tools to monitor and measure your online and digital marketing achievements.

Finally, *International marketing* could be needed *to grow your business.* International marketing is likely to be a medium/long-term strategy for most entrepreneurs, start-ups and small businesses. However, by trading overseas there is an opportunity for marketing that you may realise more quickly than you think. There a couple of key marketing issues that you need to deal with; firstly, you have to ask yourself, how am I going to actually get into a foreign market? Secondly, you need to work out which approach is best to actually get into the market.

Each of these sections has been written with you in mind, and your idea, start-up and small business. Your book uses plain language to deliver approaches, and each section uses relevant examples, which are supported by hints and tips. Enjoy your marketing journey!

Chapter 2 You and marketing

As an entrepreneur, start-up or small business person, it is likely that you bring some marketing expertise or experience with you which can generate marketing opportunities. You might have worked in sales and marketing, although it is more likely that you have consumed products and services and have knowledge and understanding of marketing from a purchaser's perspective. Either way, it is unlikely that you'll be starting with absolutely no marketing experience, or rather 'experiences.'

The purpose of this section is to identify marketing opportunities based upon your previous life experiences. Such opportunities should generate cost effective marketing, which can be undertaken with relatively less effort and resources than a fully blown marketing campaign. You are looking for some 'quick wins' which will give access to markets and sales, and more importantly, will give you some feedback on your early marketing operations. This learning can be exploited for later marketing activities.

Effectual reasoning, and marketing.

Effectual reasoning is a term coined by Saras Sarasvathy and her colleagues when considering entrepreneurship. In this chapter, let us remind ourselves, we are considering *You and Marketing* and certainly not everything entrepreneurial. We are going to audit your marketing opportunities based upon you as an individual. So, we are adapting and focusing effectual reasoning on your marketing.

Do not concern yourself with the ins and outs of the term 'effectual reasoning.' The following sections will extract everything useful, and you can take these ideas forward with you when you start marketing.

1. Start with what you have already: skills, experience, resources

- At the bottom of this section will be some examples of how individuals, with varying degrees of marketing experience, can exploit skills they already have. This is about you and your skills, experience and resources focused upon marketing activities. At the end of the section you will be given the opportunity to record these in more details, but Let us begin by asking some straightforward questions.

- What are your current marketing skills? Are you an able planner? Then you can write an outline marketing plan. Are you good at drawing? Then you can design logos. Are you creative? Then you might undertake some basic branding. You can design a marketing theme or campaign.

- Do you have some existing experience of marketing? Have you ever worked in sales and marketing? Have you organised a promotion? Have you ever organized a social or community event? Are you creative? Think about your past and how you have had some involvement in marketing. If no is the answer to some of the above, think about your experiences of marketing on a day to day basis. What products or services do you buy, and how are they marketed? What impresses you the most? Can you adapt your marketing to reflect what you have learned as a consumer?

- Do you have any marketing resources? Think about people that you know. How much money do you do have to spend on your campaigns? Do you have any materials which you could use or adapt in order to do marketing, such as paper and pens, envelopes and so on? Do you have any equipment which can be used for marketing such as printers, current websites, or friends and relatives that could do this for you?

2. Set an 'affordable loss', not a goal for gain

- A notable point about effectual entrepreneurship is that instead of having goals for profit, an entrepreneur works out how much he or she could afford to lose. This is known as an affordable loss. Therefore, work out what it is worth investing in terms of time & resources whilst not overstretching yourself, by spending time to generate marketing benefits in the medium term. Therefore, it may appear as if you are making a loss in the short term, whilst delivering benefits for the future.

3. Entrepreneurs 'recognise, respond to and reshape opportunities as they develop' by staying flexible

- A key point is that you must keep on learning as you undertake your marketing activities. Yes- it is important to be consistent with your Marketing Communications messages. However, as you develop and grow with your business, recognise and respond to new opportunities that may develop in the marketing domain. Stay flexible, and be prepared to reshape your marketing based upon what you discover on your entrepreneurial journey.

4. Make partnerships with customers, suppliers & mentors to generate knowledge & get access to resources

- Partnerships and collaborations underpin effectual behaviour. Therefore, with marketing you must make partnerships with customers, suppliers and any mentors to generate new knowledge and to get access to resources. There is a section later in this book on networking, and this will help you with collaboration and partnerships.
- This means working with customers as partners in your marketing activities. For example, you could work on a promotion together. If you decide to use a local printer or a small marketing agency, try to develop your business together as the years go by. There needs to be mutual synergy which delivers benefits for both of you.
- As you start your new business, it is likely that you may have business mentors to work with you. Use their contacts and abilities to help you develop your marketing campaigns. Ask them for their advice, and for their feedback on any campaigns which you develop.

5. Do not worry about the competition: you're probably first, new, different & innovative

- The effectual approach to entrepreneurship is likely to say that you would not really worry about competitors, simply because it is likely that you have a new and different product. If this is the case, then perhaps your marketing will reflect that. If you intend to compete in a very dynamic and busy market, then you really do need to take into account the actions and marketing of your competitors. Later sections of this book will show you how.

Let us audit your personal marketing opportunities

Effectual entrepreneurs audit themselves to establish who they know, what they know, and who they are (in terms of personality). Let us think about you and your marketing opportunities in relation to the same theory headings. Ask yourself these three questions: who do you know? what do you know? who are you? The following sections will give you a framework for assessing this. There are examples below, and it is recognized that some people will have plenty to say under these three headings, whilst others just starting out in life, may have just one or two points to make. Either way, it is important to start auditing your own personal marketing opportunities because this will save you money and resources in the future. Let us get started.

Who you know?

a) Your contacts e.g. social media: LinkedIn, Facebook, Twitter. The People that 'you know' are an important source of communication for you. This may be networking individuals that are attending a networking event; it may be personal social media whereby you communicate with people who are friends and relatives; you might use a professional network such as LinkedIn to communicate with potential customers or previous colleagues. Do not be afraid to speak to contacts because they will be a cost effective and focused way of communicating about your product or service. They may help you with your marketing because of marketing skills, or other marketing contacts that they can put you in touch with. On the other hand, try not to take advantage of people's good nature and keep people as friends and contacts. It is important to keep contacts rather than switching them off.

b) Communities of interest, sports, team mates, alumni, mentors and educators. Groups of people will also be potential sources of marketing opportunities. If you remember the club are a sports team, then informal discussions might generate some marketing leads. You can also trying get in touch with all classmates, mentors or teachers who are potentially willing to help to spread the good news about your entrepreneurial idea, or start-up.

c) People you have met. Obviously, those key contacts which you stay in touch with will be contained within your LinkedIn or Facebook profile. Nevertheless, there are people that you have met through work or informally who would be pleased to help you.

d) The strangers in your life. These are simply people with whom you might have daily or weekly contact; you might even say hello to them. However, they are not classed as contacts. Use your judgement, let us think about people who might be interested in helping you communicate the benefits of your product or service, or whom might even work in the marketing industry themselves. The idea is to turn the strangers into operational contacts.

e) Friends and family. There may be members of your friends and family will be delighted to hear about your entrepreneurial idea. Ask them if they're willing to help you to market the product; maybe they work in sales and marketing themselves, and they will give you access to their knowledge and contact base.

What you know?

a) Prior knowledge and education. Have you ever studied a topic at school or college which involved marketing in some way? Perhaps you studied a course where you worked in a team and devised a product or service to market.

b) Knowledge from your jobs. Have you ever worked in the business in or a marketing or sales function? Have you ever worked in a business which had a sales and marketing function, whereby you can contact people who were previous colleagues to offer some assistance?

c) Knowledge from your life. Have you ever designed posters, or been involved in the creative side of work? Have you undertaken a marketing campaign at work, or for a community or social based business? Perhaps you wrote articles for a magazine or worked as a DJ on a hospital radio station. Most of us have had some time in our lives when we've worked in a communications role.

d) Informal learning. It is amazing how much you pick up through your tacit knowledge, and as individuals we may have learnt some basic marketing skills by communicating with friends and family, or people at work. For example, going for an interview is a piece of personal marketing.

e) Hobbies and interests. Do you have a hobby or interest which will help you undertake the marketing for your business?

f) Sports. Will the participation in sports teams and groups give you access to people to talk to about your product or service? Will they communicate to others about your product and service?

Who you are?

a) Tastes, preferences. Your tastes or preferences are likely to impact upon your branding and Marketing Communications. Remember that marketing is about focusing upon the needs of your customers, rather than your own preferences. However, your own personality will inevitably reflect in your marketing.

Is there anything about your tastes or preferences that could be exploited in terms of marketing? If you're a connoisseur of wine, then marketing food and drink can be tailored to your own personal tastes and preferences.

b) Values and passions. Are there any values or passions which you can embed in your marketing planning? For example, if you're passionate about language or green issues, then these will inevitably feed into your marketing communications.

c) Ambitions. If you are ambitious as an entrepreneur, or you are equally ambitious for your product or service to succeed, then tell people the whole story. Make it a key part of your narrative, and build it into your marketing communications.

Examples of what you know, who you know and who you are.

Examples of what you know, who you know and who you are, based upon varying levels of life experiences. Everyone is different and each one of us will have a different profile. Do not get too concerned that if your profile is overfilled, or incomplete. This is a starting point for marketing and its design to generate some basic ideas to generate some cheap and effective opportunities for marketing.

1. A recent graduate.

Who do you know?

- You will have met plenty of people at university. It is far more likely that as a recent graduate you will have a number of Facebook friends, and a growing list of LinkedIn contacts. Hopefully you will have kept in contact with other alumni as well as teachers from your university or college. How can they help you with your marketing?
- As a younger person, you will have social friends and contacts that you have met. You may have been the member of a sports team, and you will have teammates. Friends and family will be keen to help you with your new venture. How can they help you with your marketing?

What you know?

- You will have your degree, as well as other qualifications. It is likely that you will have had a part time job whilst studying, and this will have given you the soft skills that you need as an entrepreneur. Did you run any promotions, or were you involved in any sales?
- Whilst at university, did you get involved in any business projects? What learning can you count on to help you with marketing?

Who are you?

- What are your tastes and preferences in relation to the things that you enjoy? How did you socialise? What music or movies do you like? Do you read books? What ideas can you gain from these activities to help you with your marketing?
- What are your passions? Do you enjoy sports? By evolving politics? What marketing activities are involved with your passions?

2. A woman or man returning to work

Who do you know?

- You have made a whole series of friends and contacts whilst at work before you had your family. You may or may not have a part time job, whilst bringing up your family, or you will have met people daily who may be potential influences. Get in touch with old colleagues or customers. They will remember you, and they will be willing to help. Who did you meet that were friends of your children or their parents? Socially, you will have got on with people and they may be willing to help you with your marketing. Think about networking your local business community at networking events. How can these people help you with your marketing?

What you know?

- What is your previous level of education? Did you study theoretical or practical topics? If you have not studied before, you will have developed lots of new skills whilst bringing up your family. You can delegate; you can manage time; you can organise others as well as yourself; you manage money and other or resources around the family; you can drive a car and operate equipment. How can these skills help you with marketing?

Who are you?

- What are you passionate about? Do you have an interest in animals? Do you have an interest in the environment? Do you appreciate great architecture? Are you interested in space science? You need to think about what is important to you in terms of your passions. How do your passions open doors in terms of marketing? Can you market yourself?

3. An experienced business professional

Who do you know?

- Is likely that you've made many contacts through your business experience. Hopefully you will have kept many of these concepts using LinkedIn? If not, it may be worth spending time brainstorming a core of useful individuals who you've met in the past, I'm looking for them on LinkedIn and using the Internet. If there were good friends in the past, you stand a good chance of them wishing to help you out now. A word of caution though, some people may not be interested and you'll have to live with that. However, rekindling some old mutual experiences and business deals can often remind your contacts that you are a trustworthy and professional person.
- You too, will also have friends who you have gained through sport, education and even bringing up your own children

perhaps. How can all these contacts help you with your marketing? It is likely that you will have to prioritise

What you know?

- Your business experience is likely to be beneficial to your marketing. If you have undertaken sales and marketing in a previous existence, you can use all those skills in your new venture.
- You may also have had a business education and training in previous roles.
- In business, there is plenty of informal learning taking place. You will have tacit knowledge that you have built up over your years in industry.
- You may also have hobbies and interests. Perhaps this is how you've started your business? Again, how will all of these things that you know, and skills you have developed, help you in marketing?

Who are you?

- In your business life, and in your family life, you will have had the opportunity to develop tastes and preferences of your own. However, these inform your business, and how will you use them to help you to do your marketing?
- You too will have your own passions and values. Apart from a solid business acumen, what other passions and values do you have? Is this how you started your business? Again, how will passions or values help you develop marketing?

What you know, who you know and who you are. Now it is over to you . . .

What you know?
Who you know?
Who you are?

Who can you collaborate with?

Now you have considered the opportunities that are presented by who you know, what you know and who you are, you need to evaluate whether these people or opportunities will be able to help you with your marketing. We now enter the realms of collaboration. Collaboration means working with other people, and in this instance, using them to help to market your entrepreneurial idea, start-up or small business. Such collaborations will help you to:

- Develop internal and external networks
- Engage with other businesses and society as a whole
- Develop your product ideas
- Look for cost effective ways to market your product, service, concept or idea (referring to later sections), more specifically in regard to pricing, promotion, distribution, product

development, people and staffing, using assets such as buildings or vehicles to communicate, and looking at the process of marketing for touch points whereby you can communicate your marketing benefits to customers. There will be more in later sections about this, but for now consider ways to collaborate with others to build your marketing opportunities.

Who can you collaborate with?

Are you a creative thinker?

One excellent and effective way of undertaking marketing at a relatively low cost, is to use your own abilities as a creative thinker. This next section will consider approaches to creative thinking that you might exploited in relation to your marketing. For example, you can use creative thinking to develop branding; you can use it to develop Logos and the creative feel; you can use it to develop an original concept or creative theme which can underpin all of your marketing. Creative thinking, by yourself, might even develop into a business culture that you can exploit as you grow your company, or launch your products or services.

Traffic lights. A tool for creative marketing.

Traffic lights is a simple and effective approach. It is just like the **traffic lights** that are seen in millions of streets throughout the world, and is a basic metaphor for red, amber and green.

Red means 'Let us STOP it,'

Amber means 'PROCEED WITH CAUTION, but make some improvements,' and

Green means 'Go' or 'Let us carry on with this activity.'

Traffic lights is a creative marketing tool that can be used in a number of ways.

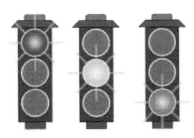

- You could conduct a personal traffic lights exercise based upon your own personal or professional development.
- The exercise can be run at any stage of the marketing planning or creative process. So, you could run it as you begin marketing, during a marketing campaign, and at the end of a marketing programme as you review or control your marketing activities.

Traffic lights has a number of benefits to marketers:

- It encourages a creative approach to marketing
- Traffic lights is simple to use
- Traffic lights is quick to learn
- Traffic lights cross cultures, since most countries use this common approach to traffic control.
- Traffic lights transcend interdepartmental and disciplinary differences so that it is a common platform for decision-making.

The starting point is to decide upon an activity on which to base your traffic lights exercise. In your case, you will be launching a new product or service, selling an idea, or growing your small business. So, try to establish a number of key questions or problems which you as an entrepreneur need to address. Select the most important handful, and then run a traffic lights exercise.

Traffic Lights, Example – Serendipity

So, let us consider a company called Serendipity that markets Ski Wear. Serendipity conducted a traffic lights exercise upon its core marketing activities. Marketing managers and interested individuals from purchasing, sales management, finance and R&D met in a training room, and recorded their views under the headings red-amber-green. The results are as follows:

- Get rid of any distributors that favour competitor brands over our own.
- Withdraw product lines that make a loss.
- Remove our branding from any non-ski wear clothing.
- Stop sponsoring amateur or low-ranking skiers, and enhance the exclusivity of our brand.

Amber – PROCEED WITH CAUTION, and make some improvements.

- Reduce the number of distributors that have Serendipity agency agreements. Start backing our proactive winners that really wish to endorse our brand and make it central to their business.
- Promote or reposition products that are mature.

Green – Go or Let us carry on with this activity.

- Reward our best distributors, and develop as the bases for long-terms relationships.
- Develop and enhance products that are highly profitable.
- Let us continue to sponsor top skiers that enhance our brand values.

You and your traffic lights

What are your problems/issues?	
Red – STOP	
Amber – PROCEED WITH CAUTION, and make some improvements.	
Green – Go or Let us carry on with this activity.	

The restaurant game. A tool for creative marketing.

The restaurant game (Green 2008) is an exercise that you can use as a student in order to generate some interesting and innovative creative ideas. The basis of the restaurant going is that you think of your product, concept or brand as a restaurant, and you ask yourself a series of questions about the restaurant. It starts like this:

- What is the product?
- What is its service?
- What is its price?
- Where is it located?
- How is it promoted?
- What is the customer experience?

So, you would answer these questions as if your idea, start-up or small business were a restaurant. It is that simple. Let us have a look at a couple of examples. Remember, you are using restaurant a *metaphor* and not suggesting a new restaurant concept.

The Facebook Restaurant, Head Chef Mark Zuckerberg.

If Facebook was a restaurant, what would it be like?

Facebook is a social networking service launched on February 4, 2004. It was founded by Mark Zuckerberg with his college roommate and fellow Harvard University Eduardo Saverin. The website's membership was initially limited by the founders to Harvard students, but was expanded to other colleges in the Boston area. Facebook has more than 2 billion monthly active users as of June 2017. It was once a start-up, with an entrepreneur with vision and ambition – just like you!

1. What is the product?

The product is social media experience. Individuals stay in touch with friends and keep them up to date with their activities. You can post messages, pictures, and so on. Facebook is immensely popular all the way around the world, it is currently free, although Facebook markets pay-per-click advertising and there are products and services which you can subscribe to. It is perceived as being a highly valuable company, although it often faces criticism because of privacy issues. The Facebook restaurant serves food (its product), which is simple and appeals to most people. It is tasty, value for money and it is shared with friends.

2. What is it service?

The service provided in the Facebook restaurant is efficient. It is quick and easy to use, and the restaurant itself is clinically hygienic. This is a fast food restaurant. It is not à la carte and everybody gets the same level of service regardless.

3. What is its price?

The food in the Facebook restaurant is very competitively priced. Pricing strategies would include value strategies, and economy pricing.

4. Where is it located?

The restaurant would be located in primary areas, and the Facebook logo would act as a call to arms for any of the global Facebook customer population. There would be a lot of customer walking past the doors of the Facebook restaurant that might drop in on impulse.

5. How is it promoted?

Obviously, promotion would be through word-of-mouth and reputation. The Facebook restaurant would not use mass media such as TV. Instead, it would invest wisely in focused public relations activities, as it did for its 2012 flotation.

6. What is the customer experience?

The customer experience would be rewarding. Customers would spend a lot of time in the Facebook restaurant, maybe more chatting and socialising rather than spending money on food. You would not get to know the maître d' and the experience would not generally be a personalised one. You would go again, and you would recommend it to friends. However, the Facebook restaurant is currently very fashionable. Marketers need to ask themselves how long this will last?

You and your restaurant (metaphorically speaking, of course)

What is the product?	
What is its service?	

What is its price?	
Where is it located?	
How is it promoted?	
What is the customer experience?	
Add your own questions.	

Conclusions

In this section, you have recognised the importance of 'You' and marketing. You have discovered how effectual reasoning can help you identify marketing opportunities, by considering the skills, experience and resources that you already have; you can set an affordable loss in the short term, and you have seen how you can be flexible and recognise marketing opportunities as they arise. You have seen how you can collaborate with others to maximise marketing opportunities through partnerships.

The section sees you and your marketing as part of one and the same. You can now audit your own personal marketing opportunities, based on who you know, what you know, and who you are. Finally, you have considered your own creativity, and how you can influence some of all your marketing activities, using tools such as Traffic Lights and The Restaurant Game. Now Let us get to grips with your idea, start-up and small business and how its advantages can be put to market.

Chapter 3 Know your customers

The fundamental question is 'why will a customer need your product or service?' If they do not need it, then it is time for a fundamental rethink. The road to entrepreneurial success is littered with great ideas that nobody needed. Failure itself is not always a bad thing, because it may be a stepping stone to future success. Nevertheless, finding out about your customer will make your entrepreneurial journey more effective. It is important to learn about your customers, to get your head around how to take advantage of what you know, and then to focus on setting some basic goals to measure success. Then you can get on with the nuts and bolts of your marketing.

15 questions to ask about your customers.

> ✍ **Describe your customers? What do you already know?**
>
> 1. *How many?*
> 2. *Where* are they?
> 3. How long do you *keep/retain* them?
> 4. What *products/services* do they buy from you?
> 5. Who are your competitors, and what can you find out about them?
> 6. Why do they buy from you and not *your competitors*?
> 7. How do you find out about *new* customers?
> 8. What are your *sources of information* about markets and customers?
> 9. Is the customer reachable? How can you reach them?
> 10. Is the market new or mature?
> 11. Is it growing or declining?
> 12. How big is the market?
> 13. What are the boundaries? E.g. overcoming problems with the law, or geography.
> 14. Is your product or service unique in any way?
> 15. Is the market concentrated e.g. local? or fragmented? e.g. international.

1. *How many?*

    If you work out how many customers you may have, then you
    will be able to estimate the size of the market and its potential
    returns. There is a concept called *segmentation* which is
    discussed in more detail in other parts of this book. So, think of
    your market as a huge orange with a number of segments. You
    may decide to target a single segment or several segments of
    the same time. This will give you the total number of potential
    customers.

2. *Where* are they?

    Try to find out how you are going to reach your customers.
    This may be to deliver a product or service, or simply to
    communicate with them. Are you dealing directly with your
    customers, or are you going to use intermediaries? Are they in
    the same geographical location issue? Are they protected by
    gate keepers in large organisations? You'll need to establish
    precisely where your customers are.

3. How long do you *keep/retain* them?

    Some organisations keep customers for a long period time, and
    nurture and build a relationship. They can think in terms of the
    lifetime value of the customer. Is this the way you wish to
    operate? Or would you have customers for a very short period
    of time ? This will dictate whether you need to keep customer
    information or learn about customers.

4. **What *products/services* do they buy from you?**

   Different customers may buy different products or services
   from you. Are you selling a range of products or services? If so
   you need to find out which customers are attracted to different
   products or services. Do they buy in bulk, or return regularly to
   buy small quantities?

5. **Who are your competitors, and what can you find out about
   them?**

   The level and nature of competition is an important area to
   investigate. Nevertheless, as an entrepreneur you are limited
   in terms of time and other resources, so you need to be very
   specific in the information that you collect about competitors.
   You could start by asking these 15 questions about your
   competition.

6. **Why do they buy from you and not *your competitors*?**

   It is important that you visit your competitors if you can. If
   they are open to the public, then experience their products or
   services as a customer would. This is important so that you can
   position your offering in relation to those of your competitors.
   Why should your customers buy from you, and not your
   competitors?

7. **How do you find out about *new* customers?**

   If you have begun trading, you will already have the number of
   customers. This is known as your penetrated market. There
   will also be a potential market of new customers that you have
   not yet attracted. Try to think in terms of the total available
   market and where to find those new customers.

8. **What are your *sources of information* about markets and customers?**

We will consider typical sources of information shortly. What is important is that the information is up to date, reliable and has relevance to your customers. Sometimes this may mean investing time or money in getting the right information. Think seriously about recording information about customers and their buyer behaviour once they become customers.

9. **Is the customer reachable? How can you reach them?**

Large sections of this book relate to marketing and digital marketing, and a key consideration is how you reach your target customers. Please see later sections of this book for specific ideas.

10. **Is the market new or mature?**

If you have a very innovative concept, then it is likely that the market is also new. On the other hand, if your enterprise is entering a current market, then it is likely that it will be more mature. If it is new, then you may be speculating on the nature of customers. If it is mature, then there will be more information about current customers and their buyer behaviour.

11. **Is it growing or declining?**

An expanding market will have more opportunities for innovation, and for entrepreneurs to establish themselves. If the market is in decline, then your product or service must offer something new which may rejuvenate the market in some way in order that it begins to expand again.

12. How big is the market?

Returning to question 1, once you know the total number of customers, you may be able to estimate the total market size. In addition, there will be other indicators in terms of market size based upon information you collect, as well as your entrepreneurial gut feeling.

13. What are the boundaries? E.g. overcoming problems with the law, or geography.

There may be boundaries of all sorts. There may be legal issues that you need to deal with before your product and service can go to market. For example, Uber and Airbnb constantly fall foul of laws in relation to employment. There may also be geographical distances between your customers if your market is fragmented. Try to establish what potential boundaries your new enterprise will have to overcome.

14. Is your product or service unique in any way?

Does your product have a Unique Selling Proposition(USP)? In what ways is it different and unique? It is important that you establish the features and benefits of your products and how they are different to those of competitors. Then you may make alterations to them, and use them as ways of differentiating your products. For example, you might change the way you advertise.

15. Is the market concentrated e.g. local? or fragmented? e.g. international.

If your business is concentrated to a specific geographical location, and this will affect the way you market. For example, if you have an artisan bakery near to residential flats, then local residents will buy your bread. Your marketing will be local. On the other hand, if you manufacture specialist devices for use in medical procedures, then your market will be dispersed or fragmented. This will have an effect on how you use your marketing mix.

Where to find out about customers.

We recognise that customers and consumers have needs and wants. We are now going to look at how we gather information about customer needs and want, since by satisfying these needs and wants is how we make profit. There are internal and external sources of information, and we tend to categorise basic information or data as either primary or secondary. Let us have a look at these terms more closely in the following paragraphs.

This list is by no means exhaustive. However, it gives you some basic ideas on how you can gather some information so that you can make some decisions. If you cannot find information, then you'd have to decide whether you are going to spend more time and money trying to source it, or whether you're going to run with gut feeling.

Internal and External Sources

Internal data is any data which relates to the inside of your business. There are going to be many examples of internal data which might include your current customer database, the number of employees which you have, different products which you have in stock or the state of the cash flow budget. Can you think of other examples of internal data? You might have the number of current customers, what they purchase, how often they purchase, and when they purchase.

External data is any data from outside of your business. Here we are into the realms of marketing research, which is research for the purposes of marketing. An example might be competitor price research or looking at the nature of your competitors' promotional activities. You could also look at specific market segments for demographics (which is the study of populations) and you could include the income of your target group, or the average age of your defined consumer. You might be able to find information on similar markets, and draw your own conclusions.

Primary and Secondary Data.

Your information or data is divided into primary and secondary. Primary data is data which is collected for the first time. Secondary data, or desk research, is data which already exists. Primary data is collected for your purposes only, and focuses on a particular problem which you have to solve. This might *be why are my customers going to my competitors?* It is specific to your question or problem, although it does have some negative points. Primary data is notoriously expensive, and it takes time and commitment on the part of the business to see it through.

Secondary data on the other hand is much cheaper and can be undertaken far more quickly. The downside of course is that the data may have been collected for the reasons other than for your specific problem, and it is often difficult to compare datasets that have been collected at different times and for different reasons. Secondary data could be out of date. An example might be that we are comparing the data on pension purchases in Central America. Each piece of research will be collected at a different time and have been collected in a different way, and you also should appreciate that the pension systems will be different in each country. Use your judgement in these scenarios.

You need to ask yourself:

- Is the data timely? i.e. is it up-to-date?
- Is it accurate?

- Is it complete or are there shortfalls with the data?
- Is it concise? i.e. it might be too large for us to gather any meaning.
- Can we understand its purpose or conclusions? Is it understandable?
- Is the data relevant to our problem or question?
- Is it economical? i.e. are we getting value for money?

Primary Research

There are many ways to conduct primary research. We will consider some of the most common methods:

1. Interviews
2. Mystery shopping
3. Focus groups
4. Projective techniques
5. Product tests
6. Diaries
7. Omnibus Studies
8. Online and social media research

1. Interviews.

This is the technique most associated with marketing research. Interviews can be telephone, face-to-face, or over the Internet.

1.1 Telephone Interview.

Telephone ownership is very common in developed countries. It is ideal for collecting data from a geographically dispersed sample. The interviews tend to be very structured and tend to lack depth. Telephone interviews are cheaper to conduct than face-to-face interviews (on a per person basis).

Primary marketing research is collected for the first time. It is original and collected for a specific purpose, or to solve a specific problem. It is expensive, and time consuming, but is more focused than secondary research. There are many ways to conduct primary research. We consider some of them:

Advantages of telephone interviews

- Can be geographically spread
- Can be set up and conducted relatively cheaply
- Random samples can be selected
- Cheaper than face-to-face interviews

Disadvantages of telephone interviews

- Respondents can simply hang up
- Interviews tend to be a lot shorter
- Visual aids cannot be used
- Researchers cannot watch behaviour or body language

1.2 Face-to-face Interviews.

Face-to face interviews are conducted between a market researcher and a respondent. Data is collected on a survey. Some surveys are very rigid or 'structured' and use closed questions. Data is easily compared. Other face-to-face interviews are more 'in depth,' and depend upon more open forms of questioning. The research will probe and develop points of interest.

Advantages of face-to-face interviews

- They allow more 'depth'
- Physical prompts such as products and pictures can be used
- Body language can emphasize responses
- Respondents can be 'observed' at the same time

Disadvantages *of face-to-face interviews*

- Interviews can be expensive
- It can take a long period of time to arrange and conduct.
- Some respondents will give biased responses when face-to-face with a researcher.

1.3 The Internet and digital surveys

The Internet can be used in a number of ways to collect primary data. Visitors to sites can be asked to complete electronic questionnaires. However, responses will increase if an incentive is offered such as a free newsletter, or free membership. Other important data is collected when visitors sign up for membership. Response rates are falling since so many businesses are using them to gather customer feedback, so be inventive and creative to maximise your response rate.

Advantages of the Internet

- Relatively inexpensive
- Uses graphics and visual aids
- Random samples can be selected
- Visitors tend to be loyal to particular sites and are willing to give up time to complete the forms

Disadvantages of the Internet

- Only surveys current, not potential customers.
- Needs knowledge of software to set up questionnaires and methods of processing data
- May deter visitors from your website.

1.4 Mail Survey

In many countries, the mail survey is the most appropriate way to gather primary data. Lists are collated, or purchased, and a predesigned questionnaire is mailed to a sample of respondents. Mail surveys do not tend to generate more than a 5-10% response rate. However, a second mailing to prompt or remind respondents tends to improve response rates. Mail surveys are less popular with the advent of technologies such as the Internet and telephones, especially call centres.

2.0 Mystery Shopping

Companies will set up mystery shopping campaigns on an organization's behalf. Often used in banking, retailing, travel, cafes and restaurants, and many other customer focused organizations, mystery shoppers will enter, posing as real customers. They collect data on customer service and the customer experience. Findings are reported back to the commissioning organization. There are many issues surrounding the ethics of such an approach to research.

3.0 Focus Groups.

Focus groups are made up from a number of selected respondents based together in the same room. You will need to organise your focus group, and incentives will need to be offered to make sure that people attend. Groups tend to be made up from 10 to 18 participants. Discussion, opinion, and beliefs are encouraged, and the research will probe into specific areas that are of interest to you and your business.

Advantages of focus groups

- You will participate in the research and learn from it.
- Visual aids and tangible products can be circulated and opinions taken
- All participants and the researcher interact
- Areas of specific interest can be covered in greater depth

Disadvantages *of focus groups*

- Highly experienced researchers are needed. They are rare.
- Complex to organize
- Can be very expensive in comparison to other methods

4.0 Projective techniques.

Projective techniques are borrowed from the field of psychology. They will generate highly subjective qualitative data. There are many examples of such approaches including: Inkblot tests - look for images in a series of inkblots Cartoons - complete the 'bubbles' on a cartoon series Sentence or story completion Word association - depends on very quick (subconscious) responses to words Psychodrama - Imagine that you are a product and describe what it is like to be operated or used. If projective techniques are useful to you, then you need to look into these approaches in more detail.

5.0 Product tests.

Product tests are often completed as part of the 'test' marketing process. Products are displayed in a mall of shopping center, or your friend's local store. Potential customers are asked to visit the store and their purchase behaviour is observed. Observers will contemplate how the product is handled, how the packaging is read, how much time the consumer spends with the product, and so on.

6.0 Diaries.

Diaries are used by a number of specially recruited consumers. They are asked to complete a diary that lists and records their purchasing behaviour over a period of time (weeks, months, or years). It demands a substantial commitment on the part of the respondent. However, by collecting a series of diaries with a number of entries, the researcher has a reasonable picture of purchasing behaviour.

7.0 Omnibus Studies.

An omnibus study is where an organisation purchases a single or a few questions on a 'hybrid' interview (either face-to-face, online or by telephone). The organisation will be one of many that simply wants a straightforward answer to a simple question. An omnibus survey could include questions from companies in sectors as diverse as insurance, medical and education. The research is far cheaper, and you commit less time and effort than conducting your own research.

We have given a general introduction to marketing research. Marketing research is a huge topic area and has many processes, procedures, and terminologies that build upon the points above.

Secondary Research

There are a number of such sources available to the marketer, and the following list is by no means conclusive:

1. Networking – 20 tips

Networking often involves meeting new contacts and developing existing relationships. Generally, you will attend a purposefully organised networking event. Look for general networking opportunities in your local trading area, or one organised by your trade/market association. Here are some tips to get you organised so that you make the most of your networking opportunities.

a) Research the networking event beforehand, and try to find out who will be attending. Visit their websites and try to get some insight into their businesses. Make notes.

b) Build a wide and diverse network. Reach out to others and use every networking opportunity. Target contacts and find out where they meet for networking. What's in it for them?

c) Have an elevator pitch or business summary ready; this means be prepared with few focused sentences to explain in plain language what you do and why you are networking.

d) Get there on time. Turning up early might give you chance to meet the organisers, and to meet other early-birds.

e) Be efficient and realistic. Connect with others that are useful to you now, or will be in the future. You Do not have time to connect with everyone, so Do not work the entire room.

f) Speak with others. Sounds obvious but you are there to network. Try to build rapport quickly. Have an opening question or sentence, such as t*ell me about your business, explain to me how your business works for customers* or *describe how you get new customers*. Prepare some before you arrive, especially if you are feeling nervous.

g) Do not be afraid to listen to other groups, and to join in. If you have something in common, then it is important that you begin the dialogue. Expect others to listen in to your discussion, and to join in too.

h) Have goals, but keep them reasonable and Do not spread yourself too thinly. For example, try to make 2 new contacts.

i) Dress appropriately. If smart dress is required, then dress smartly. If you Do not dress smartly as part of your business's ideology, then wear what makes you feel comfortable – within reason of course.

j) Remember, just be yourself. You are the most important part of your business.

k) Remember your business cards. Make notes on the cards themselves to remind yourself why you need to network. Only hand out your card to people that will value it; if you have rapport, then ask for a business card from the contact, and expect them to do the same with you.

l) Give a firm handshake and look the contact in the eye. Smile.

m) Get your elevator pitch or business summary ready. However, try to not turn the discussion into a sales pitch. You are not selling, you are networking.

n) Listen to your contact's elevator pitch or business summary. Ask a question to show that you are engaged and that you understand. Try to be interested in the conversations. Be passionate about your own ideas. Try not to hijack somebody else's conversation.

o) Be willing to end the conversation politely. Thank the new contact, and explain that you'd like to meet a few more people during the event. They will understand because they are attending with similar goals.

p) Perhaps you might be in a position to introduce other networkers to each other. You may form an informal mini-network.

q) After the meeting or event, review your new contacts. Follow up contacts quickly. Add them to your LinkedIn profile, or add them to your database. Make relevant notes.

r) Use social media to connect with relevant contacts. As with your business card, Do not try to work everyone. Be efficient and focused.

s) Once you have connected, develop the relationship. For example, send them a sample; ask them for a meeting, or invite them to become a customer or a supplier.

t) Why not organise your own networking event? Or, you could volunteer to support an event or networking opportunity organised by others.

2. Trade associations

It is possible that your business might have a relevant trade association. Essentially trade association is a business or sector association which had been founded and funded by businesses operate within a specific market. Your trade association could offer services such as legal advice, conferences or networking opportunities. A simple search using the search engine will help you discover your local or regional, or industry-based trade association.

3. National and local press Industry magazines

Look for your potential customers in targeted national and local press. You might find that your competitors also operate in the same way. So, if you manufacture radios for cars, then you might be looking for car magazines or radio magazines. It is straightforward. Also, a look to see where your competitors are advertising in national or local press. Contact the publisher and find out how much it costs to advertise. There may be packages which you might find more beneficial. Again, make sure that the cost of any advertising is absorbed, and that you are making a profit on activities.

4 National or local government.

Your national or local government may have initiatives which are designed to help small businesses and start-ups. Generally, this information is freely available using government websites. You will be looking for grants, investment funds, innovation activities which might generate tax relief, schemes designed to encourage businesses to be environmentally friendly, apprenticeships and other training initiatives, general tax relief, helplines, government websites, support programs run by local governments or educational establishments, programmes supported by the banking industry, and local business and education partnerships.

5. Websites, online and social media

There is a wealth of information online. As you will see throughout the advice given here, a simple search engine search will generate plenty of potential sources. Be careful here. There is a lot of smoke and mirrors when it comes to websites and social media. Many of these websites and social media profiles will be designed as a small business in themselves, to attract income. There is plenty of free stuff out there, and beware since you may be drawn into unnecessary programs which might be time consuming and expensive. Bookmark relevant websites and social media profiles, and take what you feel you need. Leave the rest because time is valuable.

6. Informal contacts

There is a whole section on networking. Networking involves both formal and informal contacts. However informal tends to mean friends and relatives, and relatives and friends of those people. It may be that a friend of a friend will be sympathetic to your small business needs, and will do a deal at 'mates-rates.' You might do the same when your business is up and running. Recommendation here is important, based upon people that you know and trust. Informal contacts may help you to increase in sales, or might be your first customers.

7. Trade directories

Most countries and markets will have some form of trade directory. Historically, these were large volumes that were held in public libraries, and contained long lists of businesses. Naturally the online world has overtaken this old practice, although there are still some trade directories which might be available online at a cost, or free of charge.

8. Published company accounts

Published company accounts give information free of charge in most instances. If you simply want to know how much profit a business has made, then published company accounts will give you this information. You might want to find out about a competitor; you might want to find out about a potential customer, or you might wish to gauge a ballpark figure about turnover within a particular market. This all depends on the legal form of the business. If the business which you are investigating is a sole trader or a partnership, it is unlikely you'll be are to find this information. However, in most countries public companies and limited liability companies are obliged by law to publish data in relation to their financial activities, to a greater or lesser extent. It may also be worth paying to get more detailed information.

10. Business libraries

Business libraries are a source of very detailed and comprehensive information. It depends on what kind of business you have and your needs in relation to secondary information. If your product is niche or highly technical, then relevant source information that you need may not be freely available. Therefore, a visit to your local university and its business library might be a solution in this scenario. It unlikely that you will be able to borrow books for example, although you can photocopy some material or you may wish to photograph it using your smartphone. You might take a pen and paper and jot down some relevant points. There is an issue with copyright, so it might be an idea and not to over indulge.

11. Professional institutes and organisations

In common with trade associations, it might be useful to contact professional institutes or similar organisations. There are national professional institutes for all sorts of professions including everything from architecture and agriculture to zoology. The institutes will be geared up with information to support members as well as material which is designed to help propagate their profession in the future. If you're a small business or a start-up, the institutes will be a good place to start to gather some background research and data into your potential target market. It is likely that you will need to be a professional member, and this might depend upon payment of professional fees or the achievement of professional qualifications. Check your professional institute's website to find out how to get involved.

12. Omnibus surveys

An omnibus survey is a way of gathering marketing research whereby you only need to buy one or two questions rather than undertaking an entire survey yourself. Data on a variety of subjects is collected during the same research interview. This is a much cheaper way of undertaking marketing research. Surveys are generally undertaken using the mail, telephone or via the Internet. It'll be useful to you if you have a particular problem or issue that needs to be dealt with before you progress with your marketing.

13. Previously gathered marketing research

This is a rich area of potential secondary data. Before sourcing it, you need to realise that the purpose for gathering the marketing research and the first place there may be different to your particular needs. However, it does tend to be cheaper than undertaking your own marketing research, and it exists so you do not have to do it. So, you save time and money. There are plenty of marketing research companies out there which will sell you their reports.

- A well-known example is Data Monitor. Data Monitor is a very large collection of current business reports on industries, markets and countries. It has data on consumption statistics, and tracks new product launches. This is a good place to start (www.datamonitor.com). There are others which focus upon specific industries.
- The Advertising Age (www.adage) There is a source for the advertising industry and it gives access to hundreds of research reports on specific issues within and affecting industries. Much of this is free.
- The ACSI (http://theacsi.or/) contains customer satisfaction ratings for thousands of firms which do business in the United States. Much of this data is available by industry and it is free of charge.
- The Harvard Business School is a source which links to dozens of other sources of data in relation to both the private and public sector (www.hbr.org)
- The Wall Street Journal Provides real time information about business and financial topics including exchange rates, stock values and other current topics. There is also an app, and some of the material is free.

14. Census data

A census is an official periodic count of a population which includes information such as sex, age, occupation, belief, and so on. It is generally collected by governments, so you will need to refer to websites which are run by your own government such as the Census Bureau in the USA (www.census.gov/data.html) or the Office for National Statistics in the UK (www.ons.gov.uk), amongst other nations of course. The data can be used for domestic marketing, but also consider considering international marketing which provides opportunities for businesses new or established, small or large. Look for similarities with your own domestic market. Look for markets in countries which are just developing.

15. Public and Government records

Governments spend time and money writing reports on the whole plethora of topics. Some of these will cost you money, whilst others will be open source and free of charge. Websites again are a good place to start.

The European Commission (EU) has a formidable collection of statistics on Europe, as well as about the individual nations within the European Union. Examples of statistics include income and wealth data, population data, economic performance data and much, much more.

Federal Statistics (USA) It contains a portal that links to many reports and data were collected by Federal agencies from a whole range of different industries and markets (www.usa.gov/statistics). Again, for international information, you might refer to the CIA Factbook (https://www.cia.gov/library/publications/the-world-factbook/) which contains the profiles of 300 countries providing descriptive statistics in relation to geography, commerce, population, history, and much more.

In conclusion.

The points above summarise the key sources of secondary data for your small business or start-up. Many of the sources are free or low cost, and you need to take this into account when budgeting. On the other hand, some data might cost you money, and you need to work out whether it is worth your while investing in the data. There are of course, many other sources of secondary information for your business, although those above will give you a good start. Beware that many sources of data and information are not robust, and that you need to proceed with caution. If in doubt, refer to publicly available, government endorsed material, or that which belongs to well-known companies. It is always worth asking, how did you gather your data? This will help you separate the wheat from the chaff.

✍ Quickly, think about your business. Give two examples of primary and secondary data, one from an internal source and one from an external source for each. How will you use findings for your business?

Having gathered data to underpin your business idea, is now time to take a general look at your business environment and your own personal traits; them will use a SWOT Analysis to do this. The analysis will help you consider your own personal and business strengths and weaknesses, and the opportunities and threats which are lying in the marketplace based upon the background research which you have undertaken. It may be that your product or service is a totally original concept, and therefore there will be little in terms of Marketing Data that you can use. On the other hand, you may be fulfilling a need for a gap in the market, whereby the data above more useful. Either way, SWOT is quick and useful.

SWOT Analysis

SWOT analysis is a tool for auditing an organization and its environment. SWOT analysis is the first stage of planning and helps marketers to focus on key issues. SWOT stands for strengths, weaknesses, opportunities, and threats. Strengths and weaknesses are internal SWOT factors. Opportunities and threats are external SWOT factors. A strength is a positive internal factor. A weakness is a negative internal factor. An opportunity is a positive external factor. A threat is a negative external factor.

We should aim to turn our weaknesses into strengths, and our threats into opportunities. Then finally, SWOT will give entrepreneurs options to match internal strengths with external opportunities. SWOT is that simple. The outcome should be an increase in 'value' for customers - which hopefully will improve your competitive advantage, and your chances of success.

The main purpose of SWOT analysis has to be to add value to our products and services so that we can recruit new customers, retain loyal customers, and extend products and services to customer segments over the long-term. If undertaken successfully, we can then increase our Return On Investment (ROI).

In SWOT, strengths and weaknesses are internal factors.

For example:

A SWOT strength could be:

- Your specialist marketing expertise.
- A new, innovative product or service.
- Location of your business.
- Quality processes and procedures.
- Any other aspect of your business that adds value to your product or service.
- You might have a new and exciting idea.

A SWOT weakness could be:

- Lack of marketing expertise.
- Undifferentiated products or services (i.e. in relation to your competitors).
- Location of your business.
- Poor quality goods or services.
- Damaged reputation.
- Lack of a clear concept or idea.

In *SWOT*, opportunities and threats are external factors.

For example:

A SWOT opportunity could be:

- A developing market such as the Internet.
- Mergers, joint ventures or strategic alliances.
- Moving into new market segments that offer improved profits.
- A new international market.
- A market vacated by an ineffective competitor.

A SWOT threat could be:

- A new competitor in your home market.
- Price wars with competitors.
- A competitor has a new, innovative product or service.
- Competitors have superior access to channels of distribution.
- Taxation is introduced on your product or service.

Simple rules for successful SWOT analysis.

- Be realistic about the strengths and weaknesses of your start-up when conducting SWOT analysis.
- SWOT analysis should distinguish between where your start-up is today, and where it could be in the future.
- SWOT should always be specific. Avoid grey areas.
- Always apply SWOT in relation to your competition i.e. better than or worse than your competition.
- Keep your SWOT short and simple. Avoid complexity and over analysis
- SWOT analysis is subjective. You wrote it and it is about you.

✍ Give some time to this exercise, maybe 2 or 3 hours. Conduct a SWOT analysis for your small business or stat-up idea. A piece of flipchart paper would be ideal for this task, or a large piece of paper or computer screen.

Strengths	Weaknesses
Opportunities	**Threats**

Once complete try to get a sense of perspective.

Rank the points.

Then give them a weighting from a total of 100 for <u>each</u> of the SWOT headings. If a single issue dominates then weight it highly. If points are more superficial, remove them or weight them with a low score.

Keep your SWOT and return to it periodically. It will provide an interesting record of your entrepreneurial journey.

How are you different to your competition?

Unless you are very lucky, it is highly likely that you will have competitors in one form or another. You may have a patent or a copyright which offers you some protection from competition to an extent, although even in these circumstances there is a degree of competition. Here you are going to ask yourself *how is your offering different to that of your competition?* In order to do this, we're going to look at your competitive positioning. Again, this is a very simple tool which will generate some very interesting and useful results for your small business or start-up.

Competitive Positioning

To get a product or service to the right person or company, a small business would firstly **segment** the market, then **target** a single segment or series of segments, and finally **position** within the segment(s). Think about an orange with many segments; each segment is a group of customers with the same or similar needs.

Segmentation

Segmentation is essentially the identification of subsets of buyers within a market that share similar needs and demonstrate similar buyer behaviour. The world is made up of billions of buyers with their own sets of needs and behaviour. Segmentation aims to match groups of purchasers with the same set of needs and buyer behaviour. Such a group is known as a 'segment'. Think of your market as an orange, with a series of connected but distinctive segments, each with their own profile.

Segmentation is a form of critical evaluation rather than a prescribed process or system, and hence no two markets are defined and segmented in the same way. However, there are a number of underpinning criteria that assist us with segmentation:

- Is the segment viable? Can we make a profit from it?

- Is the segment accessible? How easy is it for us to get into the segment?
- Is the segment measurable? Can we obtain realistic data to consider its potential?

There are many ways that a segment can be considered. For example, the auto market could be segmented by: driver age, engine size, model type, cost, and so on. However, the more general bases include:

- by geography - such as where in the world was the product bought?
- by psychographics - such as lifestyle or beliefs.
- by socio-cultural factors - such as class.
- by demography - such as age, sex, and so on.

A company will evaluate each segment based upon potential business success. Opportunities will depend upon factors such as: the potential growth of the segment, the state of competitive rivalry within the segment, how much profit the segment will deliver, how big the segment is, how the segment fits with the current direction of the company and its vision.

✍ **Quick exercise: segment the local market for:**

One: Restaurants

Two: Transport

Three: <u>Your own business</u>

List your segments.

Targeting

After the market has been separated into its segments, the marketer will select a segment or series of segments and 'target' it/them. Resources and effort will be targeted at the segment. It is like targeting an arrow or a dart; which segments of a dart board are the most lucrative to your small company as you begin? Start by aiming at the 20, then the 19, or maybe trebles and doubles. Do not waste your time trying to hit everything – you might hit 1, 2 or 3!

Positioning

Positioning is undoubtedly one of the simplest and most useful tools to marketers.

Remember this important point. Positioning is all about 'perception'. As perception differs from person to person, so do the results of the positioning map e.g. what you perceive as quality, value for money, etc., is different to my perception. However, there will be similarities. Anticipate your customers' perception, or just ask them!

Products or services are 'mapped' together on a **'positioning map'**. This allows them to be compared and contrasted in relation to each other. This is the main strength of this tool. You decide upon a competitive position which enables them to distinguish their own products from the offerings of their competition (hence the term **positioning strategy**).

You will draw out the map and decide upon a label for each axis. They could be price (variable one) and quality (variable two), or comfort (variable one) and price (variable two). The individual products are then mapped out next to each other Any gaps could be regarded as possible areas for new products. Decide upon the two most important variables for your customers; if there are many – then prioritise them or undertake more than one positioning map.

Undertake a positioning map for your own business idea:

a.   Decide upon two variables on which your business competes such as price, quality, innovation, high fashion, branding or others.

b.   List 5-10 competitors from competitors that supply a range of demographics from within your market.

List:

c.   Draw a positioning map on the flipchart paper, and be prepared to present it to the delegates.

Marketing Objectives and Strategies

You have considered your customers, and you have looked at your business' strengths, weaknesses, opportunities and threats. You have also considered your competitors, and looked at ways to position your idea or business in relation to your competition. Now Let us begin thinking about some basic marketing planning. The basic marketing planning will enable you to get on with the day-to-day tactical aspects of marketing.

You need to set yourself some objectives. The objectives will be the cornerstone of your marketing as you progress. Nothing is set in stone and you can tweak and adapt your objectives when you learn more about your business. However, for now we need to progress by setting some SMART objectives.

How do you make objectives SMART?

SMART objectives are simple and quick to learn. The objective is the starting point of the marketing plan. Once environmental analyses (such as SWOT) and a marketing audit have been conducted, their results will inform **SMART objectives**. SMART objectives should seek to answer the question *'Where do we want to go?'*. The purposes of SMART objectives include:

- To enable a company to *control* its marketing plan.
- To help to motivate individuals and teams to reach a common goal.
- To provide an agreed, consistent focus for all functions of an organization.

All objectives should be **SMART** i.e. Specific, Measurable, Achievable, Realistic, and Timed.

- **Specific** - Be precise about what you are going to achieve.
- **Measurable** - Quantify your objectives.
- **Achievable** - Are you attempting too much?

- **Realistic** - Do you have the resources to make the objective happen (men, money, machines, materials, minutes)?
- **Timed** - State when you will achieve the objective (within a month? By February 2028?)

Some examples of SMART objectives follow:

1. Profitability Objectives

- To achieve a 20% return on capital employed by August 2028.
2. Market Share Objectives

- To gain 25% of the market for sports shoes by September 2024

3. Promotional Objectives

- To increase awareness of the dangers of alcohol in France from 12% to 25% by June 2023.
- To increase trail of X vanishing powder from 2% to 5% of our target group by January 2025.

4. Objectives for Survival

- To survive the current economic uncertainty.

5. Objectives for Growth

- To increase the size of our Brazilian operation from $200,000 in 2027 to $400,000 in 2028.

6. Objectives for Branding

- To make Y brand of bottled beer the preferred brand of 21-28-year-old females in North America by February 2027.
- There are many examples of *SMART* objectives. Be careful not to confuse objectives with goals and aims. Goals and aims tend to be vaguer and focus on the longer-term. They will not be SMART. However, many SMART objectives start off as aims or goals and therefore they are of equal importance.

Your marketing strategy

Before we get to the tactical part of marketing (the marketing mix, which we cover in the next few sections), we need to consider how to design your marketing strategy. There are several ways to do this, and strategy can be a prolonged and extensive exercise. We need to be able to write basic marketing strategies quickly, and proficiently. So, let us begin by using Ansoff's matrix.

Marketing Strategies - Ansoff's Matrix.

Let us think about how you can market your products to new audiences. We're going to use Ansoff's Matrix. It is quick and simple, and one of the most useful tools that you will ever come across. Please Do not skip ahead – trust me.

Product / Market	Present	New
Present	Market Penetration	Product Development
New	Market Development	Diversification

Ansoff's Matrix (1957)

Some background. This well-known marketing tool was first published in the Harvard Business Review (1957) in an article called 'Strategies for Diversification'. It is used by marketers who have objectives for growth. Ansoff's matrix offers strategic choices to achieve marketing objectives. It is also very useful to small businesses and start-ups. There are four main categories for selection – market penetration (sell more to your existing customers), Market Development (sell more of your current products in new markets or segments of markets), Product Development (create great new products and sell them to your current customers), and finally Diversification (why not create new products for new markets, since you have got so much new business experience). Let us look at them in more detail.

Market Penetration

Here we market our existing products to our existing customers. This means increasing our revenue by, for example, promoting the product, changing the brand, and so on. However, the product is not altered and we do not seek any new customers.

Market Development

Here we market our existing product range in a new market. This means that the product remains the same, but it is marketed to a new audience. Exporting the product, or marketing it in a new region, are examples of market development.

Product Development

This is an entirely new product to be marketed to our existing customers. Here we develop and innovate new product offerings to replace existing ones. Such products are then marketed to our existing customers. This often happens with the auto markets where existing models are updated or replaced and then marketed to existing customers. In a café, you might change the menu or bring in new foods to commemorate occasions.

Diversification

This is where we market completely new products to new customers. There are two types of diversification, namely related and unrelated diversification. Related diversification means that we remain in a market or industry with which we are familiar. For example, a soup manufacturer diversifies into cake manufacture (i.e. the food industry). A café might start a wedding catering service. Unrelated diversification is where we have no previous industry nor market experience. For example, a soup manufacturer invests in the rail business. A café owner designs and markets wind powered electrical motors. You can still use you experiences of innovation and entrepreneurship.

Ansoff's matrix is one of the most well know frameworks for deciding upon strategies for growth. Have a go at one for yourself. It'll only take minutes.

✍ **Complete the Ansoff's Matrix for your business idea.**

Your choices . . .

1. Market Penetration

2. Marker Development

3. Product Development

4.Diversification – related or unrelated.

Conclusions

You now know far more about your customers. You can identify your customers by using different types of marketing research, recognising the pros and cons of each approach and the costs involved. Having gathered information about your customers, you can now tailor your offering in relation to your competition. You can set some basic objectives and develop an outline marketing strategy. You are now ready to move on to the marketing mix which is the tactical, or operational, part of marketing.

Chapter 4 Your marketing mix.

The marketing mix for small businesses, start-ups and entrepreneurs.

The marketing mix is a format which you can use to tailor your day-to-day marketing to the needs of your start-up or small business. This is the nuts and bolts of your marketing.

What's in YOUR mix?

The marketing mix is one of the most famous marketing terms. The marketing mix is also referred to as the 4Ps, or the 7Ps. The 4Ps are namely price, place, product and promotion. The services marketing mix, which is the extended mix, is called the 7Ps and includes the additional Ps of process, people and physical evidence. If your business is a service, then use the 7Ps.

Fancy some cake?

The concept is simple. Think about another common mix - a cake mix. All cakes contain eggs, milk, flour, and sugar. However, you can alter the final cake by altering the amounts of the mix elements contained in it. So, for a sweet cake add more sugar!

It is the same with the marketing mix. The offer you make to your customer can be altered by varying the mix elements. So, for a product launch, increase the focus on promotion and desensitize the weight given to price; if you have a café, focus on the 7Ps, and especially people (customer service), process (how you handle the customer's experience) and physical evidence (the look, feel and ambience of your café). For every small business, the marketing mix will be different.

Another way to think about the marketing mix is to use the image of an artist's palette. The business owner mixes the prime colours (mix elements) in different quantities to deliver a final colour. Every hand painted picture is original in some way, as is every marketing mix. So, do not copy the marketing mix of your competitors; instead, work it out and develop and improve on it. Make it your own.

Place

How do you intend to get your good or services to you customers?

Place is also known as **channel, distribution, or intermediary.** It is the mechanism through which goods and/or services are moved from the manufacturer/ service provider to the user or consumer. Give some thought to how your business premises might look, and how you will deliver the final product to your customer. Will you deliver it or will someone else? How much control will you need over your brand if you retail it, for example? As you read later sections in relation to digital marketing, you will appreciate that distributing your product leaves you with a number of alternatives.

Types of Channel Intermediaries.

There are many types of intermediaries such as wholesalers, agents, retailers, the Internet, overseas distributors, direct marketing (from manufacturer to user without an intermediary), and many others. Which approach will suit your business ideas best? The main modes of distribution will be looked at in more detail, but Do not limit yourself to a single channel. In fact, being innovative in terms of your channels to market might be part of your business idea.

Channel Intermediaries - Wholesalers

- They break down 'bulk' into smaller packages for resale by a retailer.
- They buy from producers and resell to retailers. They take ownership or 'title' to goods whereas agents do not (see below).
- They provide storage facilities. For example, cheese manufacturers seldom wait for their product to mature. They sell on to a wholesaler that will store it and eventually resell to a retailer.
- Wholesalers offer reduce the physical contact cost between the producer and consumer e.g. customer service costs, or sales force costs.
- A wholesaler will often take on the some of the marketing responsibilities. Many produce their own brochures and use their own telesales operations.
- You may buy from wholesalers yourself.

Channel Intermediaries - Agents

- Agents are mainly used in international markets. However, they exist in home markets too, for example when selling property or travel.
- An agent will typically secure an order for a producer and will take a commission. They do not tend to take title to the goods i.e. thy do not stock them as do wholesalers. This means that capital is not tied up in goods. However, a 'stockist agent' will hold consignment stock (i.e. will store the stock, but the title will remain with the producer. This approach is used where goods need to get into a market soon after the order is placed e.g. foodstuffs).

- Agents can be very expensive to train. They are difficult to keep control of due to the physical distances involved. They are difficult to motivate.
- However, an agent might reduce your overheads, and might be a quicker way to get your good or services to market with a relatively lower overhead.
- Write a contract with you agents and specify commissions and include a renewal date – just in case you want to renegotiate with an agent in the future.

Channel Intermediaries - Retailers

- Retailers will have a much stronger personal relationship with the consumer.
- The retailer will hold several other brands and products. A consumer will expect to be exposed to many products.
- Retailers will often offer credit to the customer e.g. electrical wholesalers, or car dealers.
- Products and services are promoted and merchandised by the retailer.
- The retailer will give the final selling price to the product.
- Retailers often have a strong 'brand' themselves e.g. Ross and Wall-Mart in the USA, and Alisuper, Modelo, and Jumbo in Portugal.
- Today, retailers always market online too.

Channel Intermediaries – Internet and digital distribution

- The Internet has a geographically dispersed market.
- The main benefit of the Internet is that niche products reach a wider audience e.g. Scottish Salmon direct from an Inverness fishery.
- There are low barriers to entry as set up costs are low.
- Use e-commerce technology (for payment, shopping software, etc)
- There is a paradigm shift in commerce and consumption which benefits distribution via the Internet.
- Your business will need a digital presence, albeit small or large. See the detailed sections on digital marketing later in this book.

Product

So, what is your product, or service? In other sections of this book we will consider innovation and product development. For now, let us assume that you have a product or service which is ready to go to market.

What will be your product or service?

The three Levels of a product

Consumers often think that a product is simply the physical item that he or she buys. You buy a new car and that is the product - simple! Or maybe not. Since when you actually buy a car, is the product more complex than you first thought? In order to actively explore the nature of a product further, let us consider it as three different products - the **CORE** product, the **ACTUAL** product, and finally the **AUGMENTED** product. This is known as the Three Levels of a Product. This will make it clearer to you, and help you communicate that to your customers.

The Three Levels of a Product
www.marketingteacher.com

The **CORE** product is NOT the tangible physical product. You cannot touch it. That is because the core product is the BENEFIT of the product that makes it valuable to you. So, with the car example, the benefit is convenience i.e. the ease at which you can go where you like, when you want to. Another core benefit is speed since you can travel around relatively quickly. For a café, it is the relaxation, or enjoyment of being served. It is not coffee or cake. The CORE product needs a lot of thought, because it will help you to market your ideas in the near future.

The **ACTUAL** product is the tangible, physical product. You can get some use out of it. Again, with the car, it is the vehicle that you test drive, buy and then collect. You can touch it. The actual product is what the average person would think of under the generic banner of product. In your favourite café, you enjoy the physical, tangible coffee and cake.

The **AUGMENTED** product is the non-physical part of the product. It usually consists of lots of added value, for which you may or may not pay a premium. When you buy a car, part of the augmented product would be the warranty, the customer service support offered by the car's manufacture, and any after-sales service. The augmented product is an important way to tailor the core or actual product to the needs of an individual customer. The features of augmented products can be converted into benefits for individuals.

Give the augmented product careful consideration, and here's why. Once you have sold your first product or service, at that precise moment, your customer is most likely to buy again; think about when you bought your cell phone, this is when you might also have bought insurance. How can you augment your product or service?

The Extended Marketing Mix for Services (the 7Ps)

The extended marketing mix is generally used for services. However, it can be applied to products as well, and which have some element of a service experience. Again, this will help you to refine your marketing mix so that it is precisely focused at your target customers. The three additional elements are physical evidence, process and people. Let us have a look at each one in more detail here.

Physical Evidence

Physical Evidence is the material part of a service. Strictly speaking there are no physical attributes to a service, so a consumer tends to rely on material cues. There are many examples of physical evidence, including some of the following; buildings, equipment, signs and logos, annual accounts and business reports, brochures, your website, and even your business cards.

Ambience

The ambient conditions include temperature, colour, smell, sound, music and noise. The ambience is a package of these elements which consciously or subconsciously help you to experience the service. Ambience can be diverse. The ambience of a health spa is relaxing and calm, and the music and smells underpin this experience. The ambience of a nightclub will be loud noise and bright lights which enhance this customer experience, obviously in a different way. You will need to match the ambience to the service that is being delivered.

Spatial Layout

The spatial layout and functionality are the way in which furniture is set up or machinery spaced out. Think about the spatial layout of your local cinema, or a church or temple that you have visited and how this affects your experience of the service. Functionality is more about how well suited the environment is to accomplish your needs. For example, is the seat in the cinema comfortable, or can you reach your life jacket when on an aircraft?

Corporate branding (signs, symbols and artefacts)

Corporate image and identity are supported by signs, symbols and artefacts of the business itself. Examples of this would be the signage in your business or on your website which reassures the consumer through branding. When you visit an airport, there are signs which guide you around the facility smoothly, as well as statues and logos displayed throughout the complex. This is all important to the physical evidence as a fundamental element of the services marketing mix.

There are many examples of physical evidence, including some of the following:

- The building itself (such as prestigious offices or scenic headquarters). This includes the design of the building itself, signage around the building, and parking at the building, how the building is landscaped and the environment that surrounds the building. This is part of what is known as the servicescape.

- The interior of any service environment is important. This includes the interior design of the facility, how well it is equipped, internal signage, how well the internal environment is laid out, and aspects such as temperature and air conditioning. This is also part of the servicescape.
- Packaging.
- Internet/web pages.
- Paperwork (such as invoices, tickets and dispatch notes).
- Brochures.
- Furnishings.
- Signage (such as those on aircraft and vehicles).
- Uniforms and employee dress.
- Business cards.
- Mailboxes.
- Many others . . .

Your organisation may depend heavily upon physical evidence. You need to decide how much you want to spend on it, in relation to the return that you expect. If you have got service, then physical evidence will be a vital part of it.

People

People are the most important element of any service or experience. Services tend to be produced and consumed at the same moment, and aspects of the customer experience are altered to meet the individual needs of the person consuming it.

Customer Service

Many products, services and experiences are supported by customer services teams. Customer services provide expertise (e.g. on the selection of financial services), technical support (e.g. offering advice on IT and software) and coordinate the customer interface (e.g. controlling service engineers, or communicating with a salesman). The disposition and attitude of such people is vitally important to a company. The way in which a complaint is handled can mean the difference between retaining or losing a customer, or improving or ruining a company's reputation. Today, customer service can be face-to-face, over the telephone or using the Internet. People tend to buy from people that they like, and so effective customer service is vital. Customer services can add value by offering customers technical support, expertise and advice.

Process

Process is an element of service that sees the customer experiencing your business's offering. It is best viewed as something that your customer participates in at different points in time. Here are some examples to help you build a picture of a marketing process, from the customer's point of view.

Going on a cruise – from the moment that you arrive at the dockside, you are greeted; your baggage is taken to your room. You have two weeks of services from restaurants and evening entertainment, to casinos and shopping. Finally, you arrive at your destination, and your baggage is delivered to you. This is a highly-focused marketing process. Another way of looking at this example is that there is 'end to end service support, which has enabled transactions between the company and its customers. Think about your customer touch points. How do you engage with the customer at every part of the process? Look for opportunities to market to new or potential customers at every stage.

Conclusions

Naturally, all aspects of the marketing mix are important. You will decide which aspects are most useful to you, and you will focus on them. However, start-ups tend to need early work on promotion and pricing, with an emphasis on digital. You'll need to communicate with the right customers in the right places, you need to get your pricing right, and you might take advantage of digital opportunities. That is where we're going next.

Your marketing mix.

Pencil in your ideas for your marketing mix. Which will you emphasise most or least? Make sure that your mix fits with your SMART objectives.

Your mix	Objective 1	Objective 2	Objective 3
Product			
Price			
Place			

Promotion			
People			
Process			
Physical evidence			

Chapter 5 Get your price right

Pricing sounds simple, but is likely to be one of the most confusing and tricky tasks for any small business. Let us look at a menu of different tools and techniques that we can use to make sure that we charge the right price, for the right product or service, at the right time, for the right customers. So why is pricing so tricky? Why do so many small business owners scratch their heads when it comes to placing a figure on a product or service? It is all about getting the price right!

Do not forget your costs

The price is simply what you charge for your product or service in terms of money. A word of warning here; there are many costs involved in terms of your product. There are fixed costs which will remain the same regardless of how many you sell, such as your premises or equipment. There are also some variable costs that increase as you sell more products, such as raw materials or packaging. The most important thing is to make sure that you know exactly what each unit costs; so, subtracting your total cost from your total revenue should equal your profit.

Let us have a look at some pricing techniques which can might be useful to you.

Penetration Pricing

Penetration pricing sees the businessman setting an artificially low price so that he or she can gain a large market share quickly. The idea is that once your customer has bought your product that you tie them in, and then gradually increase the price. This is a strategic way to price! Think about when you bought a new smartphone or a new satellite TV package; they start you a low price, right? When their customers are used to products or services, the price gradually nudges up.

Predatory pricing

Predatory pricing is very similar to penetration pricing. However, it is often illegal to abuse a dominant marketing position to incur losses through an unfair low price, which is designed to destroy competition. Be aware of this.

Loss leaders

Loss leaders are a fairer type of pricing approach; here you would price products below cost in order to attract customers. You would make profits based upon your other products with higher margins. This is often the case with retailers.

Economy pricing

This is a pricing approach where all of the added value is stripped away. Economy pricing is a no frills approach, so keep the cost of marketing information to an absolute minimum. There may be scope in your product range for an economy based product? From here you can upsell to a product or service that would better suit your customer needs, with a better margin for you. Supermarkets often have economy Brands for anything from soup to sausages. You know from your own experience that you get what you pay for, a lower price is generally for a slightly less desirable item.

Price skimming

You skim the cream from the top of the milk, right! If you are in a position where you have a unique product or a substantial advantage over your competition, then you can skim in the short term. In a nutshell, take the higher price, but expect competition to be hot on your heels to grab some of your extra profits! Then the price will gradually drift down to its regular price (or us another pricing approach from this menu).

Premium pricing

Premium pricing has much in common with price skimming. If you have a unique product or brand, then consider premium pricing.

Basically you charge the top price for your product or services. It might be a good idea to start with premium pricing and then to lower your prices if need be. If you market luxury items, if you have a patent or copyright, then premium pricing is where you begin (and hopefully where you stay). Prestige pricing is very similar to premium pricing; unlike skimming, the high price stays in place for the life of the product, and to an extent communicates a high brand value, or copyright/patent.

Psychological pricing

This is where pricing becomes a little more devious. As a marketer, you are likely to give some thought to how your customers will buy. There are a number of techniques which come under the banner of psychological pricing, that you have been exposed to for many years as a consumer. Now is your chance to put some of them into practice. Many of them depend on emotional responses rather than anything rational, or even logical. Let us look at a few.

- Price Point Perspective (PPP) is where you simply charge a Cent less than the full dollar. For example, 99¢ and not $1.00. $9,999 and not $10,000. Can you see what is happening here? Simply by removing a small amount of money the figure looks a lot less to the purchaser. It is that simple.
- Centralisation is another psychological pricing approach. This works especially well where your consumers are in a rush, or in an unfamiliar market. So, if product A costs $10.00, product B costs $20.00 and product C costs $30.00; often the consumer will centralise at product B and $20.00. The idea here is that you place your product, or the one you most want to sell, in the position of product B.

Product line pricing

What happens when you have a whole range of products to price? Well here you would consider product line pricing. So instead of adding the margin or a percentage to each product that you sell, you think about the entire range and price it from the point of view of the customer. That would mean that some products have a better margin than others. Let us say that you manufacture picture hooks so that people can display paintings. You have 10 hooks in your range, from a tiny one the size of the marble, to your largest one which is the size of a tennis ball. The tiny one costs more to produce because its smallness makes it difficult to manufacture, whilst the larger hooks are simpler to make. However, the consumer would expect to pay less for the tiny hook and more for the large hook. Therefore, you would price as a range, maybe making a loss on the tiny hooks but making plenty more back when you sell the larger ones.

Optional product pricing

Have you ever bought a new car and paid more than the ticket price? That is because when you buy the car you add leather seats, upgrade the music system and add better wheels. These are all examples of optional product pricing. Price your basic product or service, and then have a whole series of add-ons and extras ready to market to your potential customers.

Captive product pricing.

Do you sell to a group of customers at an event or within a closed location, such as a bar? Then you might try captive product pricing. There are some moral issues which you need to consider because you are charging a higher price because your customers have no alternative. That's down to you! So, where consumers are unable to swap to a competitor, you are able to charge a much higher price. An example would be if you market umbrellas at a music festival, when it begins to rain expect to sell lots of products at an increased price.

Sell them some add-ons . . .

More obvious examples with captive product pricing would include complements for products or services; if you make razors, you charge a higher price for blades; if you sell printers, you charge a higher price for refill cartridges. You might take a loss on the original item in order to make money back from complements.

Product bundle pricing

Have you got any products that just will not sell that you need to turn into cash? Why Do not you try product bundling? Here you put together a whole series of products and charge a single price for them. The consumer perceives that he or she is getting more value from the purchase, and maybe they are! Nevertheless, you are selling less popular products together with more popular ones, in the form of a bundle. Try this pricing approach to give yourself a competitive edge online, or face to face.

Promotional pricing

Promotional pricing is one which confuses even the most seasoned small business person. What is the best way to sell a product or service without affecting its brand? How do you turn products that are not selling into cash? How would you take advantage of seasonal sales opportunities? Let us have a look at some popular choices for small businesses when it comes to promotions and how best to price.

- *Buy One Get One Free (BOGOF)* is a very popular way to promote. The thinking behind the BOGOF is that the consumer thinks that they are getting a discount, or more value for money, whereas the small business person is actually selling a product at a slightly reduced margin. Okay here is an example; a cake costs 10¢ to make and sells for $1.00. From each cake, you make 90¢. If you sell two cakes for $1.00, your cost is 20¢, and you make 80¢ from the promotion. The consumer feels that he or she has had a good deal. However, your sales increase massively based upon the promotion and all you have done is reduce your margin from 90¢ to 80¢. So, if sales increase from 100 cakes ($90 profit) to 500 cakes ($400) your promotion has been a success. There are variations on this theme too; you could offer buy one, get one half-price, buy two and get one free, and so on. Remember you are after an increase in sales, and total profit.

- *Freemium* is an approach to pricing whereby a product of service is given away for nothing i.e. It is free! Everybody loves something for nothing! This can be anything from news articles to games, which are a cost to the business but ultimately retain customers. You then charge for the premium services such as a full game or a book, as examples.
- You could offer *vouchers*, or codes that can be redeemed online. This also has the benefit that you can track new or continuing customers.
- Why not offer a simple *discount*? For example, 10% off this weekend only! Make sure that you undertake your maths here, and that you are increasing your revenue by offering a discount. Try to be more adventurous, and select different approaches.

Geographical pricing

Have you ever been to different parts of the country, or travelled abroad, and had to pay more or less for a product or service? Maybe you travel to get a reduced price? The logic here is that you do not have to charge the same price in every location. If you distribute your products there are a number of different channels e.g. online or retail, you might offer an incentive for your customers to buy one way or another. If you provide a service, and need to travel to your client, then this will increase your cost and therefore your ultimate price. If you have to deliver a product to a remote location, or to a different part of the world, you need to change your price accordingly.

International pricing

If you export overseas, you need to price for that particular market. This is probably one of the most technical areas when thinking about price.

- You need to consider the cost of distributing and marketing your product overseas.
- Currencies will fluctuate. So, if you operate within the European Union and you use the Euro, this will be less of a problem. However, if you trade from the United States, and wish to trade in France, then you need to take into account exchange rates
- What price is the international customer willing to pay? What is local competition charging, more or less?
- Do you need to take into account any local taxation or government policy?
- In these situations, it is best to consult with your domestic government and take advice on international trade.

Value pricing

When times are tough, you may consider value pricing. This is a mixture of economy pricing and bundling. So, to stick with our MacDonald's example, the company has value meals which include a burger, fries and a drink at a reduced price. Consider value pricing for the shorter term, and when things improve swap to another pricing policy.

Auctions

You may decide to sell your product or service at an auction. An auction might be online, using sites such as eBay or similar, or it could be held in an auction room. With your auction, you need to set a reserve price for your product, and remember that there are often fees involved and that the final price will include a commission to the auctioneer which you will have to pay. This is also the situation when you sell online, so make sure that you know about commissions and charges and factor them in to your selling price.

The Going Rate

The going rate is where you price with your competitors. This is a really straightforward way to undertake pricing. For example, if you are a plumber, and your competitors are charging $100 as a call-out fee, then you also charged $100 if you are called-out. There is often no need to discount your prices when you can simply take the going rate.

Cost plus pricing

This is also a really popular way to price products. If your product costs $1.00 to make and you want to make a 25% margin, then sell your product for $1.25. It is a basic, but straightforward way to price your products. The downside to this pricing approach is that you might be under charging your customers! What is the point in adding 25% when your customers will pay 200%? You are not in business to give away money (although it is really great to make some friends along the way!).

Pay what you want pricing

This might sound ridiculous! In effect, you let your customer pay what they feel the product or service is worth. This could be nothing at all. However, after deeper investigation, perhaps it is a little less risky than on first inspection. If you are a new film maker in a creative industry, or you are new to the market and have no experience of pricing, you will get some early market share and indeed some notoriety, simply by using this mechanism. Often there will be some *free publicity* involved, so make sure that you issue your media release, and use it in your digital communications as a way to engage your audience.

Loyalty pricing

A theme throughout this book has been importance of maintaining customer relationships of the highest standard; that is why people go to small businesses after all. So, the price that you charge for loyal customers may be different. In fact, the price might be different for every individual customer; so, your most loyal customer might be rewarded with the best price. This is not as ridiculous as it sounds, because you need to think about your customer in a slightly different way. Think about your customer as a **long-term commitment**. Therefore, instead of making a single sale of $1000, it is better to make 10 separate annual sales of $750. This way you make $7500 from your customer in total, over time.

Your pricing strategy.

Which approaches will you use? Select as many/few as you decide necessary.

Pricing choice	Product/ service A	Product/ service B	Product/ service C	Product/ service D
Penetration pricing				
Predatory pricing				
Loss leaders				
Economy pricing				
Price skimming				
Premium pricing				
Psychological pricing				
Product line pricing				
Optional product pricing				
Captive product pricing				
Add-ons				
Product bundle pricing				
Promotional pricing				
Geographical pricing				
Value pricing				
Auctions				
Going rate				

Cost-plus pricing				
Pay what you want				
Loyalty pricing				
International pricing				

What is the best way forward for your small business? You can use a single pricing strategy, or you can mix and match the strategies above. You might use a single strategy throughout the year and then have a sales promotion; you might launch a new product at a premium price and then reduce it as it becomes mature in the market; you might enter new markets and lower your prices in order to penetrate it. The choice is yours, but at least you can reason and justify the selection of your price.

Additional Pricing Tips

Decrease prices, do not increase them.

It is always more straightforward to lower your prices than it is to increase them. Customers will always welcome a reduction in price, and in fact this may make them more loyal and even increase your sales. The reverse is possibly true as well, since if you increase your prices customers will need to make it clear in their own minds, why you've done it; so, if costs increase, or there is some inflation, then your customer will accept a price increase; if you have got your pricing wrong and have to increase your price, a customer will be less forgiving.

What's happening with the competition?

It is always worth spending some time gauging how your competitors price their products. Would you wish to emulate your competition, or are you looking for an advantage which you can gain through using a particular pricing policy? It might be a simple fact that your competitors are using a pricing policy successfully and all you need to do is the same thing.

Reduce price as a last resort

When thinking about everything that you can offer your customers, price reductions should be a last resort. Change everything else first! Change a product or service, market it somewhere different, or more importantly promote your product or service. If these measures fail, then think about reducing price or change your pricing policy. This is often a sign that the market is mature, and potentially reaching the end of its life. So, if price competition is intense, it might be a sign that you need to consider new products or services.

The McDonald's index

When pricing for an overseas market, how do you get your price right? A tip here, is to find out how much McDonald's Restaurants charge for a Big Mac in the location where you intend to trade. If the Big Mac is 10 per cent more expensive than in your home market, then add 10% to the price.

Chapter 6 Sell yourself

As you begin your journey to success, you will need to start selling. This is likely to mean that you will go face-to-face with customers, and you will sell yourself. This means that you will be responsible for selling, at least in the early days, and that you need to market yourself as part of the idea, product or service that you are marketing. This is where you will need structure and purpose. There is no point in going face-to-face with a customer if he or she is not going to buy anyway, or if they lose confidence in you because you do not seem prepared.

Be friendly and prepared.

A five-stage personal selling process

In addition to the chapters in this book which give tips and advice on promoting yourself, your ideas and your small business, this condensed chapter is ideal reading if you are about to head into a face-to-face selling scenario. The simple five step approach will give you a structured and clear way to approach your personal selling process. This is the five-stage personal selling process.

Stage one – prospecting

Prospecting is about finding new, qualified customers. Think about gold digging! If you visualise prospectors digging through in the ground and sifting through soil, you appreciate that a lot of hard work goes into finding very small fragments of gold; however, it is these tiny fragments which are your qualified leads. So, you need to process them to see if they have business potential, and make sure you're not wasting your time. So how do we assess our prospects to make sure that they will be potential customers? Let us have a look at a few approaches.

1. Always consider the needs of your prospect. As long as you focus on needs, you are making the most effective use of your time. Remember time is money!

2. Now you have a list of potential prospects, try to determine which products or services suit the needs best. Remember that the idea is we are building longer term relationship with customers, for therefore never sell them anything which will make them dissatisfied. If your product does not meet your customers' needs, then it is not a good idea to sell it to them because next time he or she will go somewhere else.

Find out as much as possible about your prospect

3. Again, in order to make efficient use of your valuable time, rank and prioritise your prospects dealing with any client who is most likely to buy from you first. You could also consider the lifetime income of each client in terms of value to your business, and deal with the most valuable first. The main thing is that you have a plan of action as you go into personal selling. Prospecting is the first stage of your plan.

Stage two – making first contact

Now it is time to prepare to contact your potential customers. There is a whole range of approaches to contacting clients, and as with prospecting you need to use the best form of communication to meet your customers' needs. Again, this may be a single approach or a use of multiple channels.

- Email. Make sure your email is short and concise and that it is tailored to specific client.
- Social media. If your business has social media, then make sure that it is simple for you to communicate directly with customers. Again, make sure that communications are created for individual clients, and Do not appear too 'spammy' (i.e. designed for a bulk audience).

Communicate using your client's preferred medium

- Letters. The personalised letter is likely to be more effective than a personalised electronic communication. It says to the client that somebody has taken the time and effort to produce something original in order to communicate with them. For important potential clients, try letters before social media and email.
- Telephone. Telephone is still a personal way to deal with clients in real time. Clients can ask questions and make alterations to an appointment in one single communication. It may be difficult for you to have direct contact with a client by telephone, and sometimes there will be gate keepers who put

obstacles in your way. Try telephone first, and then go back to other approaches.

Preparing for your sales call

So, you've been successful in securing an appointment with your potential customer. Perhaps you're at a trade show or networking event, and you're ready to sell to customers. It is time to get yourself ready for this face-to-face meeting.

- Turn up for your meeting slightly early so that if there are any delays you will be on time. Ask itself, how do you feel when people turn up late for your meetings? Always be on time.
- Set yourself some objectives; they Do not need to be too onerous, and you need to make sure that you are using your time most effectively, and that you're not wasting your customer's time. Some examples would be to sell a product or service, to develop and nurture a relationship, to inform your client of a new promotion, to close a deal is part of the process of negotiations. Never say things like 'I was in the area' or 'I had another appointment that was cancelled' because it says to your client that they are not important enough to do business with.

Always be prepared!

- Before you go to the call, make sure you've done some secondary marketing research; in other words, find out as much as you can about the client and her needs before starting the call. This information might be about the company's background, about your client's background, you might get information from the company's website with information from press releases or corporate reports. It may just be a simple Internet search about your client. You might find information from postcode data, which will give an indication of wealth or attitude. The key thing is, do not go in cold if you can find simple information quickly.

- If this is the first time that you have met the client, send information beforehand. This might be a link to a website, or a leaflet or brochure. It is likely that the customer would undertake some preparation too and if you have provided background information, this makes the process far simpler.
- Do not forget your samples and your visual aids! Let the product or service do the talking. Look for an opportunity to demonstrate your product or service, or take pictures or videos with you.
- As you begin the meeting, or the sales call, quickly state the purpose of the meeting with the customer. For example, 'today the we are going to discuss service,' or 'Let us find out which product best suits your needs in terms of items Z.' Again, time is valuable, and you want to demonstrate to the client that you're not wasting his or her time.

Stage three – the sales call, or the sales presentation.

The sales presentation is the active part of the selling process. This is where you use a variety of tools and techniques to sell your product or service to the client. There are some really interesting approaches here, and try and take a few of these with you the next time that you are undertaking some personal selling. In fact, the next time that you are buying something from a salesperson, take into account some of their tools and techniques that they employ, and ask yourself 'how effectively were they used?'

1. As you set out be as enthusiastic about your product or service as possible, but also be realistic and honest. If you are not positive about your product or service, do not expect your client to be!

2. This is a really important point, there is a difference between 'benefits' and 'features.' For example, a car has many features such as alloy wheels, digital radios, sports packages, etc. However, as a purchaser the benefit might be that the car is economical, or that it is cheap to insure. Your task is a salesperson is not to list features, but establish benefits. This is done through the use of questions, and questioning techniques are a valuable tool in the salesman's armoury. Remember, you are looking for the benefits of your product or service to your customer.

3. Questioning techniques. As a rule of thumb, let the clients do at least 80 per cent of the talking. The other 20% is you speaking, and more importantly questioning. With personal selling, the 'gift of the gab' may or not be useful. It is great that a salesperson speaks confidently and with ease; however, selling is more about getting the client to speak. Ask yourself, have you ever been put off by a salesperson speaking too much? Did it increase or reduce your confidence in the product or service?

Be prepared with focused questions

We will consider a couple of useful techniques for questioning in the sales presentation. Open and closed questions are a quick and easy to learn. Open ended questions will begin with the words when, why, what, who, where and how, or the 5Ws and 1 H. By starting your sentences with these words, the client will begin to talk; therefore, you will need to listen to the answers carefully to ascertain what benefits might add value to your clients' needs. Obviously closed questions reduce the opportunity for your client to speak, and often attract an answer of 'yes' or 'no.' By using a mixture of open and close questions, you control the conversation; so, you can speed it up or slow down, and you can move the balance of the conversation between yourself and the customer.

Another useful tool is TEDs, which is an acronym for 'Tell me about,' 'Explain to me,' and 'Describe to me.' They are open ended questions which are useful in the sales scenario to get a conversation going, or to probe a particular problem that the customer might have; again, so that you can consider which benefits might solve a customer's problem.

Stage four – objection handling.

Objections are simply obstacles that the customer puts in your way during the sales conversation. Have some techniques ready to handle any objections which your client might introduce. Objectives themselves vary in their nature and level of difficulty, so some will be easier to overcome than others. Sometimes the clients may have no intention to buy, and on other occasions customers may simply dislike you for no obvious reason. You need to put these down to experience! There are a number of tried and tested approaches to objection handling, so Let us have a look at a few here.

1. Simply try to anticipate an objection before it arises. This will come from experience; the more you hear a particular objection and handle it, the better you will get at it.

2. Try the 'Yes but . . . 'or the 'Yes and . . .' technique. Here you are being honest by accepting the objection, and you're simply diverting it. So, a client might say that he or she feels that product X is too large, and you help might respond by saying 'yes and its size makes it more robust and solid.' In one way, you have turned a negative into a positive by using this approach.

How will you handle an objection about your prices?

3. Use a TED to get the client to tell you 'why' he or she has raised this objection. This gives you an opportunity to listen to the problem in more detail and then allows you time to overcome it. For example, 'Explain to me why delivery on Tuesday is a problem?'
4. An interesting approach is to 'restate' the problem; this one works really well right out! For example, if your client says that service A is over-complicated, then restate it; 'So if you feel that our service is over-complicated?' Then if the client does not elaborate perhaps try to mix in a TED.
5. Finally, you may wish to contradict your client or customer. Be careful here, because perception in the mind of the consumer is reality. Be tactful and be respectful and try and support your answer with some informed reasoning.

Stage five – closing the sale

Closing the sale is the final stage of the sales conversation. Let us make one thing clear, sometimes you may not be able to close the sale whilst you are face to face with a client. You need to make a judgment call here, is it best to close the sale whilst I am face to face with a client? Or is it best to remain on good terms with a client and seek an opportunity to sell to them, and close in the future. One thing is for sure, to try not to make it too obvious and try not to be too pushy.

1. Why not just ask for the sale? For example, 'Would you like to buy product X?' Though it may sound oversimplified, often successful sales people get to the end of this sales process, and then forgets to ask for the order. Remember your objectives!

2. Look for buying signals. Buying signals are simply body language or the comments made by the client that they may be about to place an order. So, your customer might ask about the availability of a product or service, they might ask about the final price of the product or service, or they may just simply ask you to recap on some of the points that you made earlier. This is an indication that they may be about to buy something from you, so get ready with your final closing approach.

3. You might use the 'summary' close. The summary close is easy, but effective. Here you review the client's needs discussed during your sales conversation and connect them with the benefits of your products or services. Then you recount them as a summary. Watch your customer's reaction as you go through each point and look for agreement. Then Do not forget to ask for the order!

4. You might also use the 'alternative' close. One distinguishing factor about the alternative close is it doesn't give the customer a chance to say no. Again, use this one tactfully because you Do not wish to make this too obvious. It actually forces the client to say yes, so proceed with caution. A straightforward example of this would be, 'do you prefer the item in blue or green?' or 'would you like to collect on Thursday or Friday?' You should be fairly sure that your client

would choose one or the other before using the alternative close, otherwise it might come over as being rather cheeky.

That was the five stages of the personal selling process. You can use this as part of a very structured and planned sales presentation, or you can break it up and use it less formally as part of the sales conversation, for example when a customer enters your stand at a trade show. Try to practise each of the individual elements and find out what works best for you.

So why is personal selling more advantageous than other approaches?

It is best to use personal selling in face to face scenarios, either as a stand-alone approach or supported by other forms of marketing communication such as Social Media Marketing or mail shots. It does have its benefits:

1. Whilst personal time is a cost to your small business, it does take fewer resources than other forms of communication. Prices are often negotiated face to face, where you can have an impression of your client's body language and ask them direct questions.
2. Use this approach where your product or service is fairly complex i.e. Whereby you need to explain it to your customer. Examples may be a Financial Services business, or a technology- based business. Also, if the product or service is relatively expensive or involves the exchange of large sums of money, a face-to-face meeting is more appropriate. If your product is very innovative, you will probably need to explain it to people face to face.
3. A face-to-face sales presentation or meeting is a great way to start an ongoing business relationship. Businesses are based upon relationships, and your client will see how you operate.

On the other hand, if you have a mass market product, a simpler product or if you need to communicate with a large number of potential customers, try using other approaches in the first instance at least; then maybe you could use personal selling to close the deal. Otherwise try using a different approach to marketing promotion.

Conclusions

So how did it go? Personal selling is a learned skill, and you will get better at it. Reflect on what went well and what did not. How can you change or improve your approach in future? Did you talk too much, or not enough? Did you sell anything? Either way, just put it down to experience; learn from it and make changes for your next sales call. You will get better.

Having read this chapter, now make some notes on your personal sell process:

Five Stages of Personal Selling - My Plan
Stage one – prospecting
Stage two – making first contact
Stage three – the sales call, or the sales presentation.
Stage four – objection handling.
Stage five – closing the sale

Chapter 7 Promoting and advertising your start-up

There are many tools and techniques that will be useful to you when communicating with the outside world. Think about these tools as another type of mix, let us call it the promotions mix! Again, you will balance and blend these approaches to suit your business' needs best.

Ask yourself 'why?' are you trying to communicate with your customers, and what are you trying to say? The whole purpose behind promoting your small business is to persuade your customers that your product or service has value to them, and more importantly to build long-term relationships with customers. How you do this is down to you.

There will be some trial and error, and unfortunately you may invest in some promotions which deliver less than you invest. You will learn from your mistakes and develop effective promotional tools that suit you and your customers best.

A note about digital marketing

This chapter will consider many tools available to the entrepreneur, start-up and small business owner in order to undertake a compelling promotional campaign. Naturally, digital techniques are vital as part of any campaign. You will need to integrate all of your digital marketing activities with your regular traditional promotions. That means that everything must be consistent including your message, logo, colours and feel.

Digital marketing techniques will be explored in more detail and have a number of chapters dedicated to them later in this book. Please read on, or jump forward.

Which promotions work best for you?

How do you select the best approach? There are a number of factors that you need to take into account when selecting the best way to promote your products or services. Let us take a look at a few of them:

Cost. Of course, if you have bottomless pockets you can do plenty of promotion. Therefore, you need to look at what are expected returns based upon your communications. Do not overspend! Look for ways that you can get your messages across by spending as little as possible. That's just good business.

Your target market. The promotional tool that you select should be the most suitable one for your target market. For example, if you have a local business, then the local advertising will be better; that would include local newspapers, local Pay-Per-Click (PPC) advertising, local billboards, local sponsorship, and any approach which will directly hit your potential customers.

Availability of communications. Not all promotional tools will be available to you. There may not be a local radio station in your area for example. A particular keyword in relation to Pay-Per-Click may be too expensive simply because your competitors are willing to pay more for it. More on this later.

Look for innovation. Always think to yourself, how can I get some really effective marketing promotion by spending as little as possible? It might be as simple as sponsoring a local junior football team. You could send some very targeted e-mails to opinion leaders in your area that might have an interest in your product or service, and they might blog about your product. It is the role of the small businessperson or entrepreneur to look for ways of networking and maximising big bangs for small bucks.

Offline tools for promoting your small business

- Personal selling
- Sales promotion
- Advertising
- Public relations
- Trade fairs and exhibitions
- Sponsorship

With all small businesses *personal selling* is likely to be an underpinning marketing tool. Personal selling will be used for every stage of the marketing process for your product or services, from the early days when you are sounding-out others about your new ideas, right up until the product is withdrawn and replaced by new one.

Do not be afraid of personal selling! Anyone can learn it, and there are many tools and techniques that can be used to make sure that you get to a sale. Let us have a look at a typical personal selling process that you can use today to sell your product or services to your customers.

The idea is that you match the *benefits* of your product, service or solution to the specific *needs* of your customers, and remember that you want to build a longstanding relationship. That might mean that you do not sell today, but you sell many products and services in the future as you nurture the relationship and maintain a dialogue with your clients.

Personal Selling – See Chapter 6 - A Five Stage Process to Personal Selling

Sales promotion

A sales promotion is a short-term incentive to get customers to buy our products or services. There are many different types of sales promotion, and we will explore many of them in the next sections. You may even design your own sales promotion which is specific to your own marketing and customers, or you can blend some of the those which we suggest below.

The most important thing is that you set yourself sales promotion objectives, and make sure that you carefully cost your tools. You undertake a sales promotion if you want an immediate boost in sales, if you want people to start trying your products or service, to get shelf space, or to begin to make them more loyal so that they buy again.

Samples

There is nothing like actually trying a product or service out for yourself; therefore, if you experience it you know what you are buying and it may make it simpler for you to achieve your sale. You could give away a free sample, or you might decide to charge a small amount to offset the cost of the sample.

The most cost-effective way of using a sample is to make sure that it is given to people or businesses that are likely to buy your product or service. Obviously, some samples are delivered door to door, are given out in stores, are sent by mail, or perhaps they are given away at trade fairs or exhibitions; this is a fairly expensive way of promoting your business. Therefore, sound advice says only give away samples to those people who are likely to buy.

If you have a service, you could give all or part of the service away for free as part of a trial. One way of making samples more compelling is to have a limited number; therefore, potential consumers or business partners will need to be proactive in order to get their sample.

Coupons

Traditionally coupons were given away in newspapers and magazines, or maybe as part of a leaflet campaign. Digital marketing has rejuvenated the use of coupons. Historically the benefit of a coupon was that you had a permanent record of your customer. Of course, digital technology means that you collect digital information about customers, and therefore can tailor coupons to their needs. So, couponing is one of the few types of sales promotion which has benefited from innovative new technologies.

A coupon is basically a certificate, paper or digital, used by the customer for some kind of saving for a specific product or service. Try couponing if you are new to a market in order to get people to try your products or services out; and equally, you might have a mature product or service that needs to an increase in sales, and coupons might be an ideal way to achieve that objective.

Try digital coupons. If you have a website, or if you have your customer's telephone number, you can easily start couponing. A coupon may be redeemed on your website, or you might text a coupon to a consumer via their smartphone. There is plenty of low cost software out there which you could exploit.

There are also couponing based organisations, such as the Groupon and www.extremecouping.com, amongst others. Groupon has the advantage of being able to target local geographical areas, so might be more useful to your small business. If you have a niche product which might have more of a national or international appeal, it is probably better to avoid the large couponing companies which are better suited to more resourceful consumer brands.

Rebates

A rebate is a cash refund. The difference between a rebate and a coupon, is that the rebates are claimed after you good or service has been purchased. There are some other rather interesting rebating techniques that you might use. For example, you may set a target for your customer to reach in terms of the cash value of products that they consume over time. Then, if your customer increases purchases from $2000 per annum to $10,000 per annum you might agree a rebate of $1000 at the end of the period. This means that you have increased your sales from $2000 to $9000! Remember to cost any promotion carefully.

Money off deals

Put simply, money off deals are where you offer a discount to customer. The benefit is that the customer sees an immediate increase in value for what they pay. Again, the money off deal can be used to get a customer to trial your product, and you will get a quick increase in sales. Be careful if you wish to create the perception of high quality, because discounting your product will diminish that image.

An alternative would be a *value pack* where the consumer buys more products, but the unit price is lower. Money off deals could also include *discounting*. You must get your costing correct here, but by attracting bigger orders you might be in a position to offer discounts.

In fact, in some markets it will be expected. It would be a good idea to work out a discount structure prior to entering any kind of negotiation with customers.

Giveaways

Giveaways, also known as premiums, are products or services which are given away free or at a low price in order to provide incentives for customers to buy the product or service. There are a number of them, let us have a look at some.

Free-in or *on-pack* gifts where a small item is attached to your product as it is sold.

Free-in-the-mail giveaways where your customer collects tokens or packaging and then redeems them for a free gift.

Self-liquidating offers which see the promotion cover its own costs i.e. the giveaway breaks even. So, your customer benefits because they get the product at a lower price. You benefit because you buy product/gifts in bulk at a lower price per item. In a nutshell, the customer purchases at your cost price plus a small admin fee. Be careful though, you Do not want to be stuck with excess stock so everything must go!

Buy-one-get-one-free (BOGOF) is where the customer gets two items for the price of one. To the consumer it feels like they're getting your product at half price, but, you simply doubled your cost price. Please go to the chapter on price for an example, as well as other creative ways to use price in your marketing.

Competitions

You might consider price promotions which would include activities such as games, draws and competitions. One benefit is that costs can be calculated fairly precisely before this type of sales promotion.

Games are one of those activities which has become far more elaborate since marketing has become digital; so traditionally a game might be a bingo card or a crossword puzzle, but today the game can be a digital activity undertaken online. Obviously, there are cost implications, since we know that simple paper-based competitions are far cheaper than their digital counterparts.

Draws would be simply a lottery style activity where customers are given a ticket with a number, and when the draw happens some lucky customer will win prizes!

Competitions, unlike draws, will need a level of skill in order to win. A competition might be a quiz on a specific subject. Whichever giveaway you decide to go for, try to keep it as focused on your target customer, and your products and services, as possible. For example, if you have a cosmetics-based business, ask questions or set tasks in relation to hair and beauty.

Loyalty Cards

Loyalty cards can be a quick and effective way of selling more products, and building your customer relationship. A simple loyalty scheme would involve a card which can be stamped every time a customer buys a particular product, for example buys a cup of coffee, or gets a haircut. Once six stamps are achieved then you can give away a free coffee, or haircut.

Loyalty cards can be far more complex and data driven. If you think of the large Brands and how they use loyalty schemes, you can appreciate the level of commitment and investment that is required. For a small business, this may not be necessary, so keep your loyalty card simple to understand, and cheap to produce.

Direct mail

Direct mail may be used in collaboration with digital communications such as e-mail or social media. However, door-drops and mail-shots may be an effective way for your company to promote itself.

We have become so familiar with email campaigns that we develop a level of blindness to the communication. In fact, we may even delete such emails before we have read them. It might be fair to say that e-mail marketing campaigns have been overused, and even abused. The old-fashioned leaflet which arrives on your customer's doormat, gives you an opportunity to present an engaging image or a catchy piece of copy which may grab the attention of a potential customer.

Think about your own situation; how many emails do you dispose of in a week, which you have not read? The well written and planned sales promotion in the form of direct mail may be a better way forward for you.

One key element is that you need a focused and targeted database with a list of potential clients or buyers; this will cost you money so make sure that there is the potential to make a profit. There are marketing research companies that will have databases which you can buy into. There will also be costs in terms of postage, production and printing. You could save money by doing the door-drops yourself if you are a local business.

Directories

There are a series of different trades directories where you can promote your small company. Often, they have paid-for digital presence whereby consumers can post comments and rank and rate their experiences of companies. An example is checkatrade.com in the UK; their business model is based upon small businesses buying advertising space online. Once a customer has experienced a product or service from your company, they will either complete a paper-based postal form, or go online and complete a survey. The final outcome is a score which summarises the views and opinions of a number of customers.

There are other places where you can advertise. Local councils or departments will have to have spaces on their websites where they recommend respectable and well-regarded businesses, often based on an inspection by local council or Government officials. These recommendations are highly sought after, and still relatively cheap too! An example in the UK, is West Sussex County Council's scheme called *Buy with Confidence*. Businesses need to comply with the set of terms and conditions, and need to go through an application process.

There are also some annual membership fees. What exists in your market or locality?

Cause related sales promotion

One way of getting your message across is to work with a local or national charitable organisation. So, if you make products for pets, why not donate to, or work with, a local pet-concerned charity. You could use their logo on your products, and you might write some copy for your website which is focused upon the great work you have done together with the charity.

Cause related marketing proliferates the corporate world today, and small businesses like yours might also benefit from such associations. You may also get the personal feeling of doing good works, and that you're putting something back into the market or locality in which trade. This will also deliver a happiness dividend to your business!

Advertising

Your advertising will direct a message to large numbers of potential customers with one single communication! A couple of simple things to remember here: firstly, advertising needs to be aimed at specific potential customers from whom you need to make a profit; which leads nicely on to secondly, advertising needs to be cost effective.

It is very easy to get drawn into expensive advertising campaigns which are over complex, and which target individuals who are not likely to buy from you. Before we consider specific types of advertising Let us look at a quick way of pencilling a plan for your advertising.

Where is the best place to advertise your start-up?

Ask yourself, why do I need to advertise? There are a number of key reasons why you might want to, and you will not always see an immediate increase in sales.

- You and your company may be trying to **create awareness** of your product or service.
- If your product or service is new to the market, then you may be searching for customers to try it out. So, the purpose of your advertising is to stimulate a **trial**.
- If you have been using your personal selling skills, you may have decided that some advertising would generate some useful leads for you. If you have employed a salesforce, the advertising would *support the sales people* in the field. It is useful for **lead-generation**.
- As part of a much bigger integrated campaign, your advertising may simply **remind**, and reinforce customers' views about your product. So, if your customers have bought previously, it might reinforce his or her view that the right product is being purchased; if a customer was quite close to purchasing a product, you may have reminded her that she needs to go and buy it.
- Perhaps the most detailed and comprehensive approach that you may take as a small business, is to undergo some **basic branding**. Branding can be very expensive and time consuming, so proceed with caution. Think about trying to

position your product and service in the mind of the consumer. You might consider endorsement by a local celebrity; you could show your product in use somewhere locally; you may have undertaken some price promotion which you wish to communicate; or you may just simply be telling your potential customers about the products and their benefits. If you do attempt some basic branding, undertake some general market research first by talking to your customers. Be consistent, and make sure that all of your advertising and promotion is integrated. Do not confuse anybody with mixed messages.

Your outline advertising plan in 7 steps.

1. Who is the potential <u>TARGET AUDIENCE</u> of the advert? These are your potential customers.
2. <u>WHAT</u> do I wish to communicate to this target audience? Tell them about your product or service, its benefits, attributes and features. Tell them about your brand!
3. Why is this message so <u>IMPORTANT</u> to them? Explain and describe why they should buy your product or service and not your competition's.
4. What is the <u>BEST MEDIUM</u> for this message to take? Which particular type of advertising are you going to use? Will you be integrating and blending a number of advertising approaches? If so, make sure that your message is consistent. How will you blend traditional and digital marketing?
5. What would be the most appropriate <u>TIMING</u>? Is your product seasonal? Will your service be bought prior to public holidays? Are there certain points in the year where your product or service is more or less popular?
6. What <u>RESOURCES</u> will the advertising campaign need? You will need money! So, decide upon a budget and stick to it. You also need time and commitment to undertake your advertising campaign.
7. How do we monitor and <u>MEASURE</u> success? It is important that you measure your return on investment in advertising. Sales is a straightforward measure. Although you could also use visits to your store; ask customers to return coupons and monitor new inquiries. Remember, at the end of the day you

are in business to make money so make advertising pay for you.

Different advertising media

- Outdoor – posters, billboards and transportation
- The press (national or local) – newspapers and magazines
- Radio
- Cinema
- Television
- Digital advertising

Outdoor – posters, billboards and transportation

Outdoor advertising, which is also known as Out-Of-Home advertising (OOH), is all advertising that your customers are exposed to when outdoors! It is surprising how much advertising you can be exposed to whilst you are on the go. You will see advertising whilst walking, or using any form of private or public transport. Once you think about it, you realise how prolific outdoor advertising actually is. The main types of billboards are posters, street furniture and in-transit.

In the UK JCDecaux is the largest provider of outdoor advertising, and there are many smaller companies, and indeed local companies. So, if you have a large budget you may decide to use one of the more established national companies, however it is more likely that you do not! So, in this scenario look for a local company with some prime sites that your potential customers will pass.

Outdoor on the cheap

Again, if this might prove a little too expensive for you, it is time to use your initiative. The key to this, is that you need to find a site which is readily passed by your target groups. So, for example you have a café near to the railway station, you might approach a homeowner that lives near to the station with property that backs on to the railway. You could pay for a sign to be pinned to their rear fencing, and offer them a small monthly fee. The homeowner will not be able to see the sign and would be pleased with the additional monthly income. So, start looking for some decent sites for your outdoor advertising. What works best for you and your customers?

Street furniture

Street furniture is an unusual term. Put simply street furniture is any fixed object which the public might use. They can be something as straightforward as a public bench. Street furniture includes many fixed objects such as street signage and recycling bins.

As an entrepreneur or small business owner you need to begin to look for street furniture which is in the vicinity of your target groups. An example might be that your customers drive past a road junction which has attractive gardens nearby, maintained by your local council. So, you might ask the council if you can sponsor the gardens, by erecting a physical sign that says so. The signs often promote you to your target customers, and also may make your business appear more community spirited. Also think about more obvious approaches such as paying for benches and chairs, or fencing.

Indoor media

Conversely, as well as outdoor media you may consider indoor media. Indoor media includes items such as point of purchase material, window displays and packaging. To get an idea of how this works, pop down to your local store and look at how the larger brands go about these activities.

Point of purchase material can include shelf talkers (which are pieces of card attached to the shelf near your product) or dump bins (which are large baskets which contain your product), as well as many other innovative ideas – you may have some yourself? Window displays are often used by retailers to promote specific products or themes.

Packaging is used not only to protect your product, but also to communicate with the consumer the features and benefits of their potential purchase. In terms of these three key indoor media, ensure that any themes and messages are consistent. You may offer them free of charge to a wholesaler or retailer, as a way to incentivise the purchase of products in bulk, from you. This will help products move off the shelf more quickly, so they can be replaced by more of the same.

The press (national or local) – newspapers and magazines

Whilst we will focus on the digital advertising in various parts of this book, the national and local press are still popular forms of media. The national and local press are a more mature form of advertising, which is still very popular with entrepreneurs, start-ups and small companies. The benefit is that publishers will recognise the type of business that you have, and recommended packages of advertising that will deliver a particular rate of exposure.

Remember to keep your wits about you because newspaper advertising is a tough business and newspaper sales people tend to be paid largely by commission, so it is in their interests to sell you as much advertising as they can. Get back to basics, and locate within your outline advertising plan; what exactly do you need from the advertising?

- Work out what **size of adverts** you want. This is usually done using column inches or centimetres. As a rule of thumb adverts at the tops of pages are more expensive than those below the fold. Adverts tend to be read more if they are on the right-hand pages, and again are more expensive.
- You tend to buy newspaper advertising by a specific financial amount for example $500, or by a length of campaign which might be a month or year.
- Your advertising might also be **seasonal**; think about your Christmas Advertising; maybe use advertising as a way to stimulate sales when business is slow at points in the year.
- Remember to **proof-read** the advert. Make sure that you have signed off any creative work and check spelling and consistency.
- If you do invest in advertising, maybe include a **voucher or a code** which the customer can use when making a purchase. This will give you a broad measure of your success.

- Advertising is **costed at a rate per 1000**. So, your local newspaper could be delivered direct to 10,000 people. If you have a small car dealership, the newspaper could estimate that 60% of the readership drive cars. This gives you a *ballpark figure* on which to base your decision of whether to advertise or not. The cost per 1000 rate will at least give you a benchmark against which to compare other forms of advertising.
- National Advertising is a more likely choice if you have a **niche product**. If you manufacture fishing flies, then you might avoid all local advertising completely. You might advertise in a national fly fishing magazine, because there you hit more of your target audience. If you sell through wholesalers, this will be evidence that you are proactive in promoting your small brand nationally.

Radio

You may be lucky enough to have a local independent radio station which is listened to by your target customers. Obviously, the benefits of any broadcast radio are that the medium is largely limited to sound and therefore is often best suited to communicating pure fact, for example when you are launching a new product or when you have a sale.

You will purchase a **series of spots** which is a package of radio adverts. A basic rule of thumb is that 1000 listeners costs about $2.00 or $3.00. So, if you want to advertise at peak time when your local station has 200,000 listeners, then your 15 second spot would cost around $400/$600. You can see that by advertising at quite a time, the cost of each advert can be much lower, for example 50,000 listeners will cost $100 to $150. A tip here is to try to get a discount for the more advertising you do; when closing a deal try asking for some free slots!

The **time of day** when you advertise will affect how many people can hear your advert. For example, peak times will be when people are driving to and from work. In comparison to other types of advertising, the actual production costs are relatively low. So, the cost of making the advert needs to be taken into account, but should be much cheaper than any video production.

Do not forget there are now many **digital radio stations**. The increasing number is due to the fact that transmission costs and production cost are now much lower than in the past; also take into account that radio stations serve specific audiences, for example classic stations, golden oldie stations, lesbian, gay and bisexual stations, and religious stations, amongst many others. Also search the Internet for any online local stations, or national niche stations that better suit your needs.

Remember you're looking for the radio stations that your customers will listen to, and not the ones that you prefer yourself.

Cinemas and movie theatres

Your local cinema or movie theatre may be the place where your local customers congregate. Similar rules apply, as with radio and newspapers above, so common sense says you need to target those movies which your customers want to see.

If you have a restaurant you may decide to advertise early in the evening so that your customers will go to your restaurant when they have watched their movie; if you have a toy store you will want to target movies that will be seen by children, and more importantly their parents.

As a creative medium, obviously cinema adverts have sound, movement and colour. The downside here is that they can be relatively more expensive to make. Therefore, work with a local production company, or even your local movie theatre, and tell them the restrictions of your budget. Adverts can be based upon a series of basic photographs and text, over-dubbed with a short commentary. Your decision will be based upon the level of your resources, and your commitments to communicating a particular message. Contact your local movie theatre to ask their advice.

Television

Since you are a smaller business, television advertising is probably a less likely option for you. Of course, as a medium you can demonstrate your product in action; so, if you are a highly innovative business, you can show the features and benefits of your concept. With the advent of channels such as YouTube and Vimeo, amongst others, you can now keep your advert for much longer, and connect it to other channels such as social media and websites.

With the advent of digital media, many TV providers now give the option of recording their programmes to be viewed at a later time. Beware of this. When viewers playback recordings they will tend to skip through the advertisement which obviously you do not want.

There are benefits too. There is a much greater number of digital TV stations, so you may find one which is local that your target customers watch, or perhaps one TV station which is directed at your clients and their hobby or interest. Advertisers are getting cleverer with the way that they actually slot ads into free digital TV, and this is something that you might want to talk to the media owner about. One thing is for sure, there are lots of opportunities out there.

Guerrilla marketing

Seller beware! Guerrilla marketing is innovative and seizes the moment. It is a controversial way of promoting your products and services. The idea is that in some way you *ambush* your customers or the media that they are exposed to, such as TV or radio. For a small business, your resources will be limited; an example would be that a celebrity or sports person visits your town or a trade show organized by your industry association. You could wear a T shirt or display a banner with details of your business upon it.

If you are more dedicated, you could project a picture of your product or logo on to the walls of a local high profile building. You could take pictures of it, and share it on social media. Check your local laws and regulations. Remember, you need to be a responsible organisation because that is the least that your customers will expect.

Public Relations (PR)

Public Relations (PR) is a rather grand sounding term. In fact, it contains many different types of promotional tool which are available to you, the small business person. In a nutshell, public relations refer to any communication you may have between your small business and its customers, or more specifically its *publics*. Public(s) is a term used because we are not actually using PR to generate a sale, we actually trying to generate some *goodwill.* We will consider Public Relations in more detail later in this book.

Organising your own campaign

Once you decide upon whether or not to run a campaign, you then have a choice of doing the campaign yourself, handing over the campaign to an advertising agency, or taking *some of the services* from an agency and then supplementing with your own time and effort. The choice is yours and it is often down to the usual simple limitations of resource, your skills and the capability of the company. It is quite possible for you to prepare your own campaign:

- PC or cloud-based software packages are ideal. You could use a simple **word or publisher package** to write copy, to spellcheck and to organize it on the page. Microsoft Office is ideal for this, and other similar packages are fine.
- **Images and photos** can be created and edited using simple packages which are often distributed with PCs and tablets.
- You can take photos using **your smartphone or tablets**, the quality is suitable for newspapers or online.
- **Videos** are completely plausible too. Try taking some short videos using your smartphone or tablet, and edit them using the software which comes with your device. If you need something more complex, try packages such as Sony Vegas which are relatively cost effective.
- If you need some guidance on how to use some of these basic software packages, YouTube is an ideal place to search for

some basic information. Generally, all the information you need is there, you just need to spend a little time gathering it.

Using an advertising agency

Alternatively, you might decide to employ the services of an advertising agency. As with any investment in your business, there are benefits and disadvantages. Advertising agencies are experienced; they have an objective view on your marketing problem; they are professionals and have contacts within media; and they do not need to learn software packages.

Conversely, advertising agencies are more expensive and they are notorious for not being transparent in terms of costs. Another issue is that if the campaign is not a success, you still have to pay your advertising agency. Careful thought is needed.

Types advertising agency.

A **full-service agency** will do creative work, buy and plan your media, undertake marketing research, and produce your campaign.

You might decide to buy **À la *carte***, *whereby you can pick and choose which services you want to buy from the agency, and supplement with your own time and effort. Also consider whether you want to use a local agency or a National Agency.*

*There are also some **industry specific** advertising agencies that might specialise in your market or consumer group. It is a good idea to shop around, and to get an idea of what of is available.*

Recruit an advertising agency

*If you do decide to use an advertising agency, then you will need to **recruit them** and there is a process for this.*

- Define your advertising objectives and the nature and level of creativity that you require

- Create a list of agencies
- Provide these agencies with your creative brief and objectives, and ask them to pitch their creative thoughts
- Evaluate the offer of each agency based upon some objective criteria
- Select and recruit your advertising agency.

The recruitment process can be **time consuming**. As a small business, you need to balance the needs for a professional advertising campaign with your own priorities. It may be something that you decide to do as your business grows.

The most important point with an advertising agency is that there needs to be some **chemistry** between your small business and their creative team. If the chemistry is missing, it is unlikely that the agency will be right for you. Maybe take the agency out for a meal and a chat before signing up. Make sure that you are happy to work with these people, and consider them an extension of your own business.

Remember to discuss **remuneration** before you commit yourself. There are a number of ways to do this; traditionally the agency will take commission based upon how much money you spend on media. So, if you spend $100,000 on advertising, and the agency takes 12%, the amount payable will be $12,000. As a small business, you will probably spend much less on advertising, so insist on paying a fee which is **agreed up front**. Therefore, if your advertising bill is $5000, agree a five per cent fee and pay $250. If you do decide to pay more for your initial campaign, make sure you keep all of the copy, images and other promotional materials. You may decide to use them again in the future with another agency, or with an in-house own campaign.

Measuring the success of your campaign

Most of us do not have the time to measure success. However, evaluating how successful your campaigns and promotions have been, is an important way to learn. Use this learning to make your campaign and promotions more effective and profitable in the future. Here are a few tips on ways to gather information on the success of your promotions.

- **Record data** from your sales calls. There is software available to do this which is relatively cheap and simple.
- For all of your customers, make sure that you keep **customer records** up to date and look for increases in purchasing during promotions.
- Measure and record any **new contacts** through telephone, e-mail or any other digital medium such as contact forms from web sites.
- If you give out **samples**, ask respondents for their basic details and contact them in the future.
- **Coupons** are ideal paper-based feedback devices. Record coupons once they are redeemed, and make sure that you offer customers the chance to opt-in to further communications.
- If customers participate in **competitions**, again ask them for their details and offer them the chance to opt-in.
- **Loyalty cards** are a fabulous way to record customer data. You will be able to see if customers buy more than promotional periods.
- If you decide to use **direct mail**, offer the respondents the opportunity to sign-up using his or her e-mail or social media.
- If you get a new contact or customer, ask them **how they heard about you**. Was it from a directory? Was it because of an advertising incentive, or sample? Do they see your sponsorship of a local charitable event or organisation? Had they seen or heard any TV or radio advertisement?
- Measure against any promotional or advertising **objectives** which you set. So, if you wanted to increase *trial*, did more potential customers try out your products?
- Always make sure that there is a **Call-To-Action (CTA)** no matter what the form of communication. A CTA is simply a website address, e-mail address, social media link or telephone

number where potential customers can contact you. This is really important.

- If you use **PR approaches**, ask questions such as how many people attended your product launch? How much of your company literature has been used and who did you give it to? How many interviews or photo calls have you done, and for whom? How many people have visited your facility, and who were they? If you have been lobbying, what has been the result?

- **Media and press releases** should also be measured. This is a simple matter of going through local or national, or trade press, to establish which publishers have picked up your message. You will know which publications have most relevance to your own ideas or small business. Also check digital media such as websites and blogs, focusing on those that serve your customers or target market.

- Measure **the attendees** at your stand when you undertake a trade show or exhibition. When you followed up, how many became loyal customers?

Conclusions

There are many traditional offline and online approaches to promotion, and this book is loaded with them. Try to make sure that you are being cost-effective. Target current or potential customers. Most important of all, you must be consistent; make sure that your marketing promotions and communications are integrated and clear.

Make some notes in readiness for your campaign.

Plan your promotions and advertising		
Promotion/adverting media	**Objective one:** e.g. *To inform engineers to support our new products*	**Objective two:** e.g. *To persuade the consumer to buy our digital services*
e.g. Technical magazines	X	
e.g. Local radio		X
e.g. Personal selling	X	X
Budget	$	$

An outline promotions plan - example

	Customer 1	Customer 2	Customer 3	Cost
January	Pay-per-click Local Press	Sales Call Email	Sponsorship	£500
February	Pay-per-click Local Press	Email	Direct mail shot	£400
March	Event Pay-per-click Local Press	Event Email	Event	£1000
April	Pay-per-click Local Press	Email	Sales call	
May	Pay-per-click Local Press	Sales call Email	Website	
June	Pay-per-click Local Press	Email	Website	
July	Pay-per-click Local Press	Email	Sales call Website	
August	Pay-per-click Local Press	Email	Local press Email	
September	Pay-per-click Local Press	Sales call	Direct mail shot	
October	Pay-per-click Local Press	Email		
November	Pay-per-click Local Press	Email		
December	Pay-per-click Local Press	Email		

Now begin to pencil in your outline promotions plan. What will you communicate to customer, when and how?

Your outline promotions plan

	Customer 1	Customer 2	Customer 3	Cost
January				
February				
March				
April				
May				
June				
July				
August				
September				
October				
November				
December				

Chapter 8 Public Relations (PR) for you

Public Relations (PR) is simply how you communicate with your public and with the media. As you launch or grow your business, you will depend upon your reputation for survival and success.

Public Relations (PR) is a single, broad concept. It is broad since it contains so many elements, many of which will be outlined in this lesson. Public Relations (PR) are any purposeful communications between an organisation and its publics that aim to generate goodwill. It is not quite the same as marketing because its more about maintaining a great public image, rather than paying for specific media.

Where marketing has a segment or a number of segments, PR has a *public* or a number of *publics*.

It is also a myth that PR is free; you need to be organised, and prepared to pay to maximise PR tools below. Consider the array of approached that follow. Some may be more useful than others; some might exploit current strengths to deliver cost effect PR. Let us take a look.

Speeches, presentations and speech writing.

Key figures from within an organisation or entrepreneurs will write speeches to be delivered at corporate events, public awards and industry gatherings. PR company officials in liaison with businesspeople often write speeches and design corporate presentations. They are part of the planned and coherent strategy to build goodwill with publics. Presentations can be designed and pre-prepared by PR companies, ultimately to be delivered by you, or you can write your own of course – much cheaper.

Corporate literature e.g. financial reports.

Corporate literature includes financial reports, in-house magazines, brochures, catalogues, price lists and any other piece of corporate derived literature. They communicate with a variety of publics. For example, financial reports will be of great interest to investors and the stock market, since they give all sorts of indicators of the health of a business. A company entrepreneurs will often write the forward to an annual financial report where he or she has the opportunity to put a business case to the reader. This is all part of Public Relations.

Publics, put simply, are its stakeholders. PR is proactive and future orientated, and has the goal of building and maintaining a positive perception of an organisation in the mind of its publics.

Yes, it is difficult to see the difference between marketing communications and PR since there is a lot of crossover. This makes it a tricky concept to learn. Added to this is the fact that PR is often expensive, and not free, as some definitions would have you believe. PR agencies are not cheap. You will need to do as much of your own PR as time allows. However, sometimes it is better to pay a small local or growing PR agency to take up your work.

Interviews and photo-calls.

It is important that entrepreneurs are available to generate goodwill for their organisation. Many undertake training in how to deal with the media, and how to behave in front of a camera. There are many key industrial figures that proactively deal with the media in a positive way for example Bill Gates (Microsoft) or Richard Branson (Virgin). Interviews with the business or mass media often allow a company to put its own perspective on matters that could be misleading if simply left to dwell unattended in the public domain.

You (the entrepreneur) will be able to communicate with local media or industry media. You could be interviewed and posted on YouTube. There are a number of ways that you could be interviewed, cost effectively.

Organising events.

This has a direct business payoff. A more informal event could include a day at the races or a short-break abroad, where clients are wined and dined at the cost of a company, in order to generate goodwill. This has an indirect business payoff. On the other hand, you might organise an event. Please see the bespoke Events section.

Sponsorship and charitable donations.

Sponsorship is where an organisation pays for their product or service to be associated with an activity or event. Organisations commonly sponsor sporting events, such as The Olympics, sporting stars and other celebrities, or medium, for example television programmes. The sponsors gain exposure, and also align their product or service with the attributes of the sport, celebrity or medium. You can sponsor local causes; Why not sponsor an event, or a local sport-team? Why not sponsor a garden or other public amenities? Again, focus on your market/industry or your locality.

Many companies (often those in profit!) make donations to charities and good causes. When donations are publicised, again the benefits generate goodwill for the organisation. It should be noted here that Microsoft's Bill Gates donates substantial amounts to good causes that are often not reported. This is true corporate philanthropy.

Corporate events are used to woo publics in both a formal and an informal manner. A formal corporate event could include a manufacturer inviting employees from all of its many distributors to visit its manufacturing plant for a training day.

Facility visits.

Visits to a factory, such as a chocolate factory, or a facility, such as a brewery, also generate a positive perception of a small business. In the case of a factory visit, loyal customers or other interested parties can experience for themselves what is behind a new product. In the case of a new facility, concerned or misinformed publics have the chance to see for themselves what really occurs behind locked doors. Here the organisation has the chance to deal with a delicate topic in a planned proactive manner.

Publicity events and 'stunts.'

Publicity events fall under the banner of guerrilla marketing. Here an entrepreneur will take the opportunity to seize upon a particular moment to hijack public attention. Publicity events and stunts are practised by both companies and private bodies (including pressure and political groups). A famous example of a publicity stunt was one conducted by Fathers for Justice (a British pressure group for divorced fathers), whereby individuals, dressed as Superheroes, invaded Buckingham Palace in London. Try to think of a way to generate interest in your own idea or small company.

Product placement in media.

This is an interesting and original use of PR. There are very many examples in movies and TV programmes that 'place' products. Is there a TV or movie producer that might like your idea and include it for free? Is it worth paying for a glimpse of your product in use by a celebrity in a movie?

For example, a car manufacturer places a car in a movie and the hero drives it, or wears a watch that is looked at by the villain displaying the time, underscored by the manufacturer's logo. Today, computer games include banners and posters during game-play as the action unfolds. Examples of product placement in games would include field sports with adverts placed alongside a pitch, or car racing games where you pass billboards displayed in a city.

Media conferences.

Media conferences are called often at short notice to inform the media directly about a current event *that has just happened*, or that is about to happen. Media contact includes interviews with key personnel, and could include speeches, presentations and speech writing by the PR company. Finally entertaining the press, or media, is undertaken when trying to gain as much media space as possible. This could be for a product launch or to promote an acquisition.

Advertorials in newspapers, magazines or on websites.

Advertorials are paid for advertisements that are designed to appear like copy (i.e. normal reported text). Many countries insist that advertorials do contain a line of text to explain that they are sponsored or placed by an advertiser. Advertorials are often used to imply that some ground-breaking treatment or solution has been uncovered.

Corporate promotional materials, websites, in-house magazines and customer magazines.

The market for promotional materials is large. Promotional materials include items such as pens, balloons, mouse mats, and so on. They tend to carry a company's logo and contact details, and are another way to promote goodwill between and organisation and its publics. Websites are a vital marketing communications and public relations tool that can convey information to publics on how to contact an organisation, key personnel, products and services, corporate history, and financial reports, as well as any other targeted and planned information. Again, see sections on digital marketing throughout this book.

In-house magazines are used for internal marketing, communication and change management from within the organisation. In-house magazines are targeted at internal publics. Conversely, customer magazines help organisations to communicate with external publics (mainly customers) on all sorts of topics such as good news stories, product launches, customer clubs and many other subjects.

Lobbying government bodies.

Lobbying is named after the 'lobby' area of the British Houses of Parliament where traditionally 'lobbying' would have occurred. Lobbying, in the past, would have meant catching the eye of a Member of Parliament, in order to persuade him or her to take up a particular cause or argument. Today, lobbying firms are hired by organisations or individuals with a specific cause to promote. For example, a charity could lobby for a change in laws regarding pharmaceuticals or armaments. The charity would hire a lobbying firm to promote their cause with elected politicians. If your product or idea might impact social change in some way, speaking to your local government representatives might be a useful way to make public sector contacts, or attract government grants.

Press or media conferences, contact and entertainment.

Press or media conferences, contact and entertainment are pivotal Public Relations strategies. In the past, the press was the original target (e.g. newspapers and magazines) but today the whole media industry forms the target (i.e. radio, websites, TV, social media, and so on). Media releases are drafted by a PR company, for example, to report financial information prior to the release of company reports.

Conclusions – Do It Yourself (DIY)?

You need to cherry-pick those approaches which are best for you. Try to be as cost effective, creative and original as possible. Always maintain integrity, and remember that PR is all about goodwill, and maintaining your reputation. As a start-up, you will almost certainly do much of this yourself, especially in the early days.

Your Public Relations plan

Complete the following PR plan, based upon your SMART objectives. Remember that you should make sure that messages are consistent with other aspects of your marketing. Do not confuse publics or customers with conflicting or confusing messages.

Public Relations (PR)	Objective 1	Objective 2	Objective 3
Speeches, presentations and speech writing.			
Corporate literature			
Interviews and photo-calls.			
Organising events.			
Sponsorship and charitable donations.			
Facility visits.			
Publicity events and 'stunts.'			
Product placement in media.			
Media conferences.			
Advertorials in newspapers, magazines or on websites.			
Lobbying government bodies.			
Press or media conferences, contact and entertainment.			

Chapter 9 Writing a successful blog for your idea, start-up or small business

If you are new to blogging, then the whole topic of writing a successful blog for your small business, idea or start-up, may seem a little daunting. This section will consider the pros and cons of a blog, and offer advice and tips on how to make your blog more compelling.

Write a blog about yourself as an entrepreneur

What is a blog?

So, let us get back to basics -what is a blog? A blog as a personal diary which is updated online. You can share your expertise, thoughts and ideas. The word comes from a shortened version of *web log* or *weblog*, hence *blog*. Originally blogs were simply places to write about your day-to-day activities, in the same way as you would do in a paper-based diary.

Some are boring and mundane! Some are not! In fact, the more interesting and absorbing blogs became so popular that the bloggers tended to make a decent living. Video bloggers, or vloggers, do the same today – in fact many of them have become thought-leaders and celebrities in their own right.

Create your own blog

- You need to select a **blogging platform** such as WordPress or Blogger. If you have built a website already, it is likely that you will be able to blog freely by simply creating a new post. If not, you will need to organize a hosting provider and a domain name (see earlier sections on WordPress).

- Add a **theme**, or skin, to your blog. This will give it a more original and authentic look.

- Once the blog is ready, and you have a theme, you can now change the look and feel of the site by using tools to alter its appearance; this will make it more **personal**.

- You can add **plugins** which are tools to enable you to undertake tasks such as adding social media, or creating mailing lists.

- The next step is to work on **quality content** for your blog. This is probably the most important aspect, and will generate a readership audience for your work.

Blogger is a free blog, from Google.

Become an expert Blogger

- Your readers will expect you to be one of the **opinion leaders** in whatever topic you write about. So, if you have a flower retail business, your readers will expect you to know all about the best way to arrange roses. Whilst there may be better qualified experts elsewhere, you are the person that your readers are following, and therefore you need to live up to the title of *expert*.

- If you are not comfortable being an expert, then **refer to other experts** within your field.

- **Write at regular intervals** and make sure that you always compose good quality content. Be reliable and post on time.

- **Case studies** are fabulous tools for you to go in to more depth, and for you to demonstrate the extent of your professional knowledge. This may mean that you need to source and gain access to a particular organisation in order to write your case study. It a good idea to obtain **permission** before you publish anything about someone else's organisation, their personal qualities, or use photos, which include themselves or their business.

- Do not worry too much about giving away things for **free**. Write compulsive, engaging and must-be-seen content that will grasp the interest and attention of your readers.

- Deliver **in-depth** material rather than superficial jargon. This will show that you have a professional knowledge of your topic, and it will help you to recruit new customers.

- **Do not** write shallow posts. **Do not** write simple lists.

- Finally, you must have a **strong opinion** or view on the topic that you are writing about. Do not sit on the fence! Do not be afraid to tell people what your view of a particular situation is, after all you are the expert.

Tips and techniques for successful blogging

- Design a **publishing schedule**, and stick to it. You do not have to write an entry every day. Find out what your readers require and how often they want it, simply by asking them.

- Begin a list of potential **blogging ideas**. There will be times when you are lucky enough to have an abundance of ideas on which to base your blogs. Take into account, that there will also be times when you work harder for ideas. Therefore, keep a list of potential blog post ideas; give some examples of what you intended to happen; use short, sharp bullets, or mind-maps to remind yourself of your reasoning in the future.

- Read as much as you can. By reading around your topic of expertise you will develop and enhance your professionalism. You may read outside of your industry area of expertise, but then draw it back again and reflect upon your blogging topic. Make sure that you've read all of the key texts, and that you are referring the main industry websites. **Keep up to date**, and the current.

- As you begin your posts, explain in short sentences exactly **what will follow**. This will entice your reader to continue reading, and will give you a structure for the post which you will write. This will prevent any aimless meandering.

- Continue with a **straightforward structure**, and Do not confuse your reader.

- **Do not** leave your writing until the last minute. If you plan ahead, then spend time working on your blog and make sure that it is a quality piece of work. If you would not read it, why should your clients read it?

- It is a good idea to keep a post in **reserve**. Therefore, if you are ill or if life takes over, you have a post ready to send out to your eager readers.

- You may be one of those people that is able to write from 8.00 AM to 8.00 PM, and you will generate some quality content. If this is you, that's marvellous. However, if you're an entrepreneur or a small business person, it is likely that you will have many other tasks to complete during your busy working days. A better solution would be to write for 30 minutes to 60 minutes, and then take a break and work on other tasks for your business.

- Staying on this topic, if you feel enthusiastic and **full of energy** and your writing is flowing, then write more blog posts! If you have something on your mind, then write it straight away providing you have the opportunity to do so.

- Go and take a look at **other people's blogs**; this will give you an idea of what makes content mundane or compulsory. Find a Blogger that is interesting, and learn to write in a similar style or technique.

- Make sure that you are focusing upon your **target audience** i.e. the people who ultimately will spend money with your business and will become loyal customers. **Do not** waste your time trying to please everybody.

- Write what **feels natural** for your audience; Do not write in hyperbole, which means to grab attention or to generate clicks. You are not in the business of getting people to click through, you in the business of retaining profitable customers.

- **At the outset**, explain exactly what your blog is about and who it is going to please. Make sure that you stick to this purpose and generate content to please your readers, and to make them loyal – of course.

- **Vary the length** of your blog posts. If you have finished saying what you got to say, then that is the end of the blog post. There is no point in stretching content because it will become thinner and less interesting to your readers.

- **Check your spelling and grammar**. If you make mistakes in your work your readers will notice it, and this will mean that they have less faith in your writing skills.

- **Include guest posts**. You may have friends or colleagues there are interested in your area of expertise. Perhaps you have employees or suppliers that work for your small business by blogging? Ask reliable writers to write blog posts, and given credit for their work.

- Include **something visual.** Try to add an image or video to support your blog post. People tend to scan posts quite quickly, and having something which is eye catching will slow down the eye, and draw them towards your content. It also important to include an image/logo for many blogging websites, so that it can be included in summaries of posts which can be found on other pages.

- Look at **your competition**. Make sure that you know what your competition is up to. What are they doing? What are you doing, which adds value to what you do? Look for opportunities to add value in terms of your blog post.

- Use **outbound links.** Once you have written your work you can include links to other websites which have examples and/or support your reasoning. Focused and relevant outbound links can improve the attractiveness of your blog post in the search engines.

- Once you have completed your blog post, go back and **proof read it**. Make sure that you chop up out any unnecessary text. Keep it focused and succinct.

- As with your social media, you need to create a **conversation.** Ask your readers some questions in your copy. Find out what they think about topics which you are writing about. Ask them for their experiences. You can even open up the comments on your blog page, but make sure that you monitor them carefully.

- **As you complete your blog post**, draw together all your themes. If you post a question in your introduction, then answer it in your conclusion based upon what you have written.

- Finally, add **internal links** to any similar blog posts that your reader may be interested in.

Conclusion

The public are generally interested to hear about new innovations. You need to promote yourself as an entrepreneur, and you can provide the narrative for your start-up using one of many free tools. Blogging is a cost-effective way of kick-starting your marketing.

Chapter 10 Organising your event

If you want to get your marketing message across to specific potential customers, face-to-face, in one place, then consider organising your own event. The following tools and tips give you advice on your approach, based upon the Five Ws and How of Events Planning.

1. **The Five *Ws* and *How* of Events Planning:**

When organising an event, you will need a process which will make your endeavour a success. By using a simple Five Ws and How approach you give yourself an overview – Who? What? When? Where? Why? and How?

2. **Who** are your guests? Who is holding the event? How many people are expected to attend? Do any of the attendees need any additional arrangements e.g. the elderly, disabled, or children?

3. **What** is your event? What sort of event do you intend to hold? Consider your attendees and what might appeal to them. Will the venue be indoors or outdoors? Discuss with delegates:

    - Live music and sport
    - Festivals and cultural events
    - Meeting and conferences
    - Incentive travel
    - Product launches
    - Exhibitions and tradeshows
    - Weddings, anniversaries and birthday parties
    - Ask delegates for others from their personal/professional network.

4. **When** is your event? What is the deadline for your event? Make sure that it will not clash with other events that your delegates may wish to attend. Does the deadline leave you with enough time to plan? How long will the event last –

hours/days/weeks, and will it be at a particular time e.g. weekend, Bank Holiday, evening, afternoon or morning?

5. **Where** is your event? Is it easy to find? Will it be local? Will it be international? Think carefully about the venue that will best suit your event and your delegates. Will you need parking? Will you need to arrange transport?

6. **Why** is this event happening? What is the purpose of the event? Does your organisation have aims and objectives that need to be achieved? Do you intend to sell any products; create awareness; increase knowledge; build relationships, and so on?

7. **How** much money is in your budget? When is the money available? Do you need to consider cash flow?

Do not forget!

All successful event organisers need to consider other relevant supporting activities/tasks that ensure that our events run smoothly. Let us consider them in the list below, and add your own where necessary for your own specific market or customers.

8. **Checklist – Health and safety planning for an event.**

   - Have you decided who will help you with your duties?
   - Is there a clear understanding within the organising team of who will be responsible for safety matters?
   - Have you risk assessed your event and prepared a safety plan?
   - Did you involve your workers during the planning of your event?
   - Did you liaise with other agencies?
   - Have you gathered and assessed relevant information to help you determine whether you have selected suitable and competent contractors?
   - Have you provided the right workplace facilities?

- Have you planned for incidents and emergencies?

9. **Seven steps to risk assessment**

- Identify the hazards
- Decide who might be harmed and how
- Evaluate the risks and decide on precaution
- Record your findings and implement them
- Review your assessment and update if necessary
- Take legal advice if you feel that there are potential risks.
- Insurance might also be useful.

10. **Security**

- Safety stewards
- Door supervisors
- Crowd management
- VIP & corporate protection
- Brief and recruit a security company

11. **Transportation**

- How is easy is your venue to reach?
- Information about how to reach your venue from an airport, by rail, by car and by foot.
- Do you need to organise transport for your guests?
- Do you need parking permits?
- Brief and recruit a transport company.

Your Events Management Sheet

Firm up your *Five Ws and How* audit into a more detailed Event Management Sheet. Here's a template.

Name of event:		Date:			
Aim of event:		Event type:			
Start time:		Finish:			
Item		**Date**	**Who**	**Complete**	**Notes**
Budget					
Write budget					
Budget signed-off					
Guests					
Which people?					
Agree numbers					
Confirm guest list					
Agree final numbers with venue(s)					
Venue and Location					
Agree event location					
Create a venue checklist					
Generate running order					

Shortlist and visit potential venues

Get quotations

Determine final venue

Undertake Health and safety audit.

Undertake Risk Analysis

Pay deposit

Pay balance

Speakers and entertainment

Arrange technology e.g. music, screens, WIFI

Prepare/check speeches

Book speakers/entertainers

Catering

Own or venue? Confirm.

Source caterer

Confirm caterer

Confirm menu/drinks

Arrange for licenses

Pay any deposits

Confirm final numbers

Pay any balances

Technology/lighting/audio visual

Own or venue? Confirm.

Source company

Obtain a quote from supplier

Confirm company and agree quote

Pay any deposits

Pay any balances

Marketing

Draft text and artwork

Agree text and artwork

Printing

Online/e-mail

Networking

Social media

Distribute invitations

Send RSVP reminder

RSVP cut-off deadline

Security

Develop a security checklist

Source company

Obtain a quote from supplier

Confirm company and agree
quote

Pay any deposits

Pay any balances

Venue set-up

Develop a checklist for venue
set-up

Arrange access to venue

Supply running-order to venue

Print names badges

Organise an administration
desk

Event follow-up

Develop a clean-up checklist

Clear venue

Follow up with
visits/letters/emails to guests

Send thank you letter/emails
to helpers

Check that all accounts have
been paid.

What could be improved next time we run an event?

Chapter 11 Getting started with your digital marketing

Digital marketing for entrepreneurs, start-ups and small businesses

Digital marketing is ever-changing. If you are part of the generation of people who has grown up with technology, you will undoubtedly find the challenges of digital marketing exciting and stimulating; if you have not, then the anticipation of embarking upon digital marketing will possibly be more daunting.

Digital marketing is fundamental

This chapter offers a practical approach to digital marketing. It will show you how to do the basics, such as simply registering an account, as well as offering you advice and tips on how to supercharge your digital marketing activities.

The chapter will focus on topics including:

- Your online advertising
- Pay-Per-Click (PPC) advertising
- The Google AdWords program. Paid-for advertising.
- Google's Small Business services, most of them FREE.
- Affiliate marketing
- Viral marketing
- Google Analytics, for measuring success
- Google Webmaster Tools

Also take a look at other chapters in this book which consider Your Social Media, E-mail marketing, Get Online (Websites and online stores), Search Engine Optimisation (SEO) and measuring your online success.

Your online advertising

Online advertising is likely to be central to any digital marketing undertaken for products or services, and provides a whole series of opportunities for entrepreneurs, start-ups and small businesses. There is lots of choice. Therefore, obey the usual rules of marketing such as where do our customers congregate online, what will they be searching for and how can I get in touch with them online? Naturally, take control of costs and make sure that you get plenty of bangs for your bucks. There are still some real opportunities for focused and cost-effective online advertising. Let us take a look at them now.

Pay-Per-Click Advertising (PPC)

The majority of online advertising today is conducted using a Pay-Per-Click advertising (PPC). If you look at the top of a Google search, you will see a series of the adverts before the actual search engine results appear. Here's an example of a search for 'cheap+pianos.'

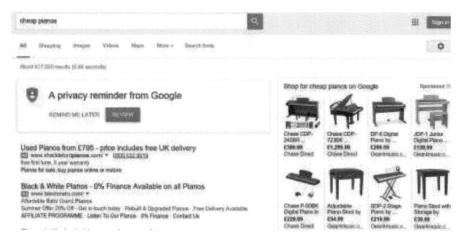

Try a simple search 'cheap+pianos'

Google AdWords

These are paid-for adverts using a product called Google AdWords. There are a number of competitors which are also available including Bing Ads, although Google AdWords is by far the biggest player in the market.

Notice how the top section of the search results displays the term 'Ad' in a box. On the right-hand side are some images of pianos, with prices and links to the advertiser. These advertisements are all paid for. The benefit to the small businessman is that there is no charge to display the advertising as with traditional media, such as TV and press. You do not get charged until somebody **actually clicks** on the advert – hence the term Pay-Per-Click (PPC). The more you are willing to pay for your PPC advertising, the higher your adverts will appear in relation to the other companies competing for the same keywords. It is similar to an auction, but for the best position.

Google AdWords is a must for PPC

It is worth noting that just below the adverts appear links to websites which are generated through organic rankings. These are websites which have content which is very closely linked to the terms typed into the search box in a regular Google Internet search. For popular search terms, these websites have worked very hard to get their high-ranking position. In fact, there will have been a lot of time and resource given to their high ranking in the search engine. This is also down to popular and precise content, supported by SEO. It would be a mistake to think that it is simpler to try to get to the top of the search, especially for popular terms.

A simple AdWords example

There follows a more advanced explanation, but put simply – you bid for a series of *keywords* such as 'cheap+piano' 'budget+piano' 'bargain+piano.' Prices can vary from a few cents to many dollars.

Let us say your keyword 'bargain+piano' cost 10 cents per click. You pay in advance, using your company credit card. You buy $100 worth of advertising which is 1,000 clicks. Again, in basic terms, you sell 5 pianos, and generate 500 new members for your mailing list, as well as a new distributor. You can cost the pianos – you may make a margin of $100 per piano = $500 income. Bingo! You've made $400 additional income, 500 new mailing list customers for your 'funnel,' and a new business partner – the latter being less measurable. You can see why online advertising provides such an opportunity.

AdWords – getting started

Signing up for Google AdWords is very straightforward. You simply start an account, and if you get stuck you can telephone a Google advisor to help you. You can tailor your advertising to suit specific customers, and you can change your advertising campaign throughout the year. You are able to measure the impact of your advertising, and you can make changes to improve it. Basic data will explain to you how many people saw your ad, and then went on to click your ad. You can make alterations to improve the rate of click through. You can set a daily budget limit when you sign up, and you can change it at any point.

AdWords – simple steps - Let us do it.

1. **Sign up** at www.google.com/adwords (or your local equivalent e.g. co.uk/AdWords)

Google AdWords   Already a Google AdWords customer? Sign in

Overview   Benefits   How it works   Costs   Testimonials   Get started

Ready to get started?

You can sign up online today. Or if you invest £5 a day or
more, our team of experts will help get you get set up and
optimise your campaign.*

Sign up yourself

Get started in minutes

Follow a few online steps to open your account. Then just write your ad,
choose your keywords, set your budget and you're finished.

Get expert support from Google

Off to a great start

Sign up for an AdWords account 1

2. **Create your advert.** Tell your customers what you have to offer. Choose your search terms (keywords) such as 'budget+piano'. Set your daily budget – keeping it low at first. A popular keyword will scoop your investment quickly. Hence, explore cheaper, niche keywords. They do exist, and Let us face it, if nobody clicks on them, you pay nothing.

3. Your potential **customers will see your advert** when they search for similar terms e.g. 'where can I buy a budget piano?' Your advert will appear! Google does this automatically.

4. **Customers click** on your advert, and they go to your website. The cost of the click is deducted from your daily budget.

5. Whilst this might sound like the end of the journey, **it is actually the beginning**. There are a number of actions you can now take to improve your customer acquisition and retention. Let us look at some of these.

   • Once the potential customer has entered your website, you need to make sure that the page that they land on has all of the information and images that they will need to make a decision.

   • Also make sure that there is a **Call To Action (CTA)** which means a button for them to click on, a telephone number for them to call, a shopping carts to begin the ecommerce process or some dynamic operation which will lead your customer to the final sale.

- Now you have started your **AdWords journey**, you can change and improve the adverts themselves so that more clients click on the advert and come to your website. Therefore, you can also change your web pages to make sure that as many people buy your products as possible.
- If people do not buy, you need to *grab* **their data**. Put simply, you have gone to a lot of time and effort to get potential clients to come to your website. If they decide to leave without buying, you have lost contact with them. Use a mailing list or some incentive, such as free information or a free trial or a sample, to get the person to sign up with your website. This means that you can market to them in the future and close the sale a different day. Do not just let them walk out of your store, not now.

6. **AdWords has a learning curve.** You will get better at it with practice, and it is highly likely that AdWords will become part of your daily marketing online. If not, invest a small amount at first and if it does not work for you, you can put it down to experience without losing too much cash.

Google Small Business

Google Small Business is a **YouTube channel** which helps small businesses to succeed on the Internet by connecting them with each other as a community, and with Google's own experts. It a really interesting place to find some easy to use advice about how to succeed using the Internet. Simply search for it on YouTube. You can find it here: www.YouTube.com/user/GoogleBusiness

Google Small Business is a community, supported by Google's experts.

Why Google?

Google is the top of the food chain when it comes to Internet searches. However, this well-known global digital company also has many free tools for the small business person. Google My Business is a free service whereby you can register your correct information about your business with Google itself.

Claim your business

You can maintain and update your business information online. You can either add your business to Google, or you can claim it. Begin by searching for your business on Google and click on the link which allows you to claim your business. Alternatively go to www.google.com/business and login, or sign up for your Google account. Once you login, you can search for your business; if it is there you can claim it; if it is not there you can add it. Once you have added your details and you are happy with them, you then need to verify the information. This involves Google sending you a special code, which arrives at your business address. Simply log on to Google and verify your information using the code. This might take a few weeks, so be patient.

An example of how your business appears when it is claimed/registered as a business with Google.

Affiliate marketing

Affiliate marketing is a route to market for your small business. Put simply, you sell digitally through a partner. Affiliate marketing is a process where a small business attracts customers by rewarding some third parties, known as *affiliates*, for marketing their goods and services, and/or for driving traffic to their website. It feeds your digital marketing funnel by driving potential customers to your website or social media, or it markets and sells products on your behalf.

Affiliate example – Amazon.com

Develop your own affiliate program

A straightforward example from the corporate world, would be that of Amazon. If you have a website about hunting and fishing, and you attract and retain many visitors who associate themselves with these hobbies, you can become an Amazon affiliate. Amazon is the *merchant*. You are the *affiliate*.

What would this entail? You would need to go to Amazon's website and sign as an affiliate. Then you can search for the books and other products which are suitable for the hunting and fishing fraternity. Having selected suitable products, and here is the clever part, you cut the relevant code from Amazon's website and paste it into your own pages. Then it will look as if you have a series of products to sell to your visitors, in the same colours and livery as your own pages. However, once the customer decides to buy the products, he or she is rerouted to Amazon's own website. They take payment from the customer and supply the goods; you, as the affiliate, will receive a commission. Other than that, you do not participate in any part of order fulfilment. This is a simple affiliate process.

Your own affiliate program

Why not consider your own affiliate programme? You would be the merchant (as Amazon was in the example above)

Benefits of affiliate marketing, as a merchant.

- everything is *tracked* and so each stage can be checked by the merchant and the affiliate; this means that both parties are accountable. You pay for performance. If there is no action, there is no cost to you. The action could be a sale, a click-through to your site, or some market information, such as a completed survey.
- your costs are fixed. You specify what results you require, and the payment is fixed.
- access to many different industries, *new segments* and markets both nationally and internationally means that merchants gain access to channels quickly. Market expansion is a key reason to use affiliate marketing.
- marketing to new channels, especially *international markets* tends to be time-consuming and fairly risky; affiliate marketing is less risky than comparable modes of entry into new channels and overseas markets. Affiliate marketing is lower risk, because you do not pay if it does not work.
- Affiliates use their own skills and resources to market your products and services.

Set up your own affiliate program

If you decide to set up your own affiliate network, then there are a number of things you need to take into account. There will be some costs involved for your small business to manage the affiliate program, for the platform itself i.e. software and digital marketing, and for creative costs for design, look and feel. Essentially you have two choices, to join an existing affiliate network or to install some specialized software In-house.

Using a current affiliate network is quick and simple.

The affiliate network is based upon intermediaries that drive merchants to your program. They will already have a series of merchants who would join your program and you can build a small critical mass of online distributors. Software is included and you do not need to install it on your own servers; It is all done online and you simply join the program. There will be costs involved in setting up the programme, and of course fees and commissions will be payable to merchants, as well as the online affiliate network company.

However, whilst you have control over your potential merchants, you may spend a lot of time reviewing them. If you Do not, then anybody could be using your logo and promoting your products on their website and you lose some control over your brand. Also, if affiliate marketing becomes popular for your business, software can be somewhat limiting in relation to what else is available in the market today. For comparison, potential affiliate networks include:

- CJ Affiliate
- ShareASale
- LinkShare
- Clickbank
- Clicksure

As your business grows, or if you foresee that affiliate marketing will be central to your digital strategy, specialized affiliate marketing software might be a better option. This gives you more creative freedom, and the opportunity to design your program so that it feeds your business perfectly. The software is generally more functional.

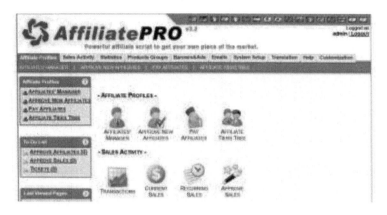

Specialized software gives more control

Specialized software does not give you access to a current successful network. It means that you start on your own from scratch. The software is largely online. It is also generally more expensive, so you will need to budget for your software provider. However, if affiliate marketing becomes popular for your business, then you will not be paying out commissions to the software provider, and therefore this solution may be more cost effective. For comparison, potential in-house providers include Cake, HasOffers and Affiliate Pro.

Viral marketing

Viral marketing is an often discussed term, but how will it help you to market your small business? Viral marketing is the equivalent of online word-of-mouth. Viral marketing, aka Buzz marketing, uses all of the digital marketing media to disseminate a message which is passed along from person to person; it is viral because it spreads like a virus or disease and if successful, communications can expand exponentially. You are not paying to spread the word as you would be in a Pay-Per-Click (PPC) campaign. Viral marketing campaigns are often spread via e-mail or social media (and here we include YouTube as well). The campaign can reach a large number of individuals in a relatively small amount of time, and this would be useful to your small company in many instances.

What makes a successful viral?

- It can be funny
- A Viral can be outrageous
- It has a unique or controversial approach
- Culture can be challenged such as gender or class
- Try something that has no connection with your product.

Keep virals small and focused

Remember, you are an entrepreneur or small business. Therefore, something which goes viral may be completely out of your control! Do you really want national and global coverage for your product or service? It is more likely that you will need some niche, or local coverage. Therefore, tailor your viral to your niche market, or your local customers. For the small business person, a viral might mean that you target five segments of your most loyal customers with your promotion - with 10 friends in each, extending your potential customer interaction to 50 people. These 50 people are more likely to be interested in your product or service, and will trust the person who recommends you. Keep your virals small and focused.

Conclusion

Digital marketing is fundamental to entrepreneurs. Review some of the digital media above, and use them to achieve your objectives. This chapter introduced you to basic information about Pay-Per-Click (PPC) advertising such as Google AdWords, Google Small Business, affiliate marketing and viral marketing. Also make sure that you watch emerging digital trends and look for new digital media opportunities as time unfolds. The following chapters include even more digital marketing and social media marketing opportunities.

Let us make a start by making some plans based on this digital marketing introduction.

Digital marketing	Objective 1	Objective 2	Objective 3
Pay-Per-Click (PPC)			
Google Small Business			
Affiliate marketing			
Viral marketing			

Chapter 12 Your website and online stores.

Demystifying digital marketing for entrepreneurs, start-ups and small businesses

Starting and running your own small business is demanding in terms of time and other resources. How much should you spend on digital marketing, and how can you spend your time effectively to get the results that you need? You may already use social media, and you might be comfortable building websites. However, the chances are that you have a little or no knowledge of digital marketing. For that reason, this chapter will take you back to basics, and give you an overall view of your business' approach to the digital world.

Digital marketing provides many choices

It is highly unlikely that you can avoid digital marketing. Therefore, you need to make sure that you Do not overdo your digital marketing, and that it is right for your target customers. As with other promotional activities, your digital marketing will need to be integrated and consistent.

You will need to decide whether you build your own website or whether you pay for the services of a professional developer. Will you need an online store? Or perhaps Amazon or eBay are more suitable for getting your products to market. Perhaps you will decide that advertising online is the best way to employ your digital marketing efforts. On the other hand, your digital marketing activities might focus on communication, and therefore, e-mail marketing will be important to your company. Whether you are a manufacturer, a distributor, professional or service provider, your website will need some Search Engine Optimisation (SEO) and in the next chapter we demystify SEO and offer some simple tips to help your website rank as highly as possible in the search engines.

When you consider that digital marketing also includes ways of measuring and monitoring your success online, and that there is an array of free tools for you to use provided by companies such as Google, then you can appreciate that as a small business person, you have a very interesting time ahead of you. Social media is likely to be an extremely important marketing tool for your company. This chapter will also show you how to get your content marketing right, so you can communicate in the right way with the right people. It will also investigate some popular social media channels including Facebook, Twitter, Instagram, Pinterest, and others. It will take you from the basics of simply signing up, to how you can plan and implement an effective social media campaign. In addition, we investigate the benefits of writing a professional blog. So, this next section is a smorgasbord of digital marketing tools and tips, so Let us get cracking on your digital marketing today!

How much digital marketing is enough?

With your digital strategy, you need to decide how much of your valuable time & resources you are willing to dedicate. In order to do this, there are a series of questions which you need to ask yourself; spend some time thinking about this because the digital world is full of smoke and mirrors. It is suggested that you undertake some basic background research with your current or potential customers. You'll be surprised how much you can find out. Here are some questions that you can ask:

1. What proportion of your target audience are using different digital platforms? Within this chapter you will explore the most popular types of websites and social media. The point here is that if your customers prefer to use Twitter then there is little point in focusing on Facebook. So, find out what your customers are using, by asking them.

2. *Which content and promotions are your audience interested in?* Once you know the preferred digital and social media choices of your customers, then review what they're looking at and try to find out which promotions most interested them. TripAdvisor is an example of this; find current clients and follow the reviews that he or she has placed. This will give you an overview of what they like and what they dislike; similarly look to see if they review car hire or transfers, or whether their comments say they have used particular promotions. What are they sharing on Facebook? Which websites are they talking about on Twitter? You can build quite a detailed image of your customers' online behaviour, which will help you plan for it.

3. *How are competitors using the platforms – benchmark what's working for them?* You may have to become a mystery shopper! It goes without saying that as a small business you will sign up to the digital communications offered by your close competitors. So, how many followers do they have on Facebook and Twitter? What online marketing are they doing using their websites? What seems to be working well for them? Then you can emulate their success, adapt it and then improve it. So, a quick audit of your competition is important.

4. *Reviewing your own analytics, sales and customer insights.* Within this chapter we will discuss online analytics and marketing research; digital marketing leaves a rich trail of data which can be used to analyse and evaluate the success of your campaigns. You need a critical mass of traffic to do this. If your digital approach generates one visitor per day, digital marketing may not be the right route to your customers, and you may prefer to use more traditional promotional methods. However, if you can grow your traffic to 10, 50, 100 or 1000 visitors per day, then you have data which can be used for analysis.

Keep it simple. If you post some interesting content and your traffic increases, then you know you have got it right. If you put effort into writing material and there is no noticeable increase in traffic, then you need to change something. You need to deal with this at a basic level. There is a lot of hot air spoken when it comes to digital marketing and you need to be prepared with some basic knowledge to help you overcome the pitfalls. **Unless you can justify a huge expense on digital marketing, do not do it!** Start small, simple and proficient and go from there.

Share your vision using digital marketing

5. Setting broad goals and vision/mission for the organisation. If digital marketing is central to your business offering, then the online experience needs to have some broad goals and a central vision. So, what is your vision? What will your business look like in five years' time? You can change your vision as time rolls out, but you need a central purpose for your online business. So, what will it be?

- Facebook's mission is to give people the power to share and make the world more open and connected. (Facebook 2016)
- "Apple designs Macs, the best personal computers in the world, along with OS X, iLife, iWork and professional software. Apple leads the digital music revolution with its iPods and iTunes online store. Apple has reinvented the mobile phone with its revolutionary iPhone and App store, and is defining the future of mobile media and computing devices with iPad." (Investopedia 2016)
- Coca Cola's mission is to refresh the world in mind, body and spirit, to inspire moments of optimism and happiness through

our brands and actions, and to create value and make a difference. (Coca Cola 2016)

6. Get more specific with SMART objectives
(specific/measurable/achievable/realistic/timed). Finally, you need to translate your vision and purpose into SMART the objectives. For example:

- To increase traffic to 10,000 visitors per day within three years.
- To have 30,000 registered e-mail addresses in your opt-in mailing list within 24 months.
- To sell 10 items per day through your online store within six months.
- To achieve 5000 Twitter followers in a single year.

Make sure that your digital marketing is INTEGRATED

It is important that you do not confuse your customers. Therefore, make sure that your digital marketing and your traditional marketing/promotion are integrated. That means they must tell the same story with the same feel, logos, colours and messages. Think of all of your marketing and advertising as a single communication.

Your website

The first place that any of your potential customers or clients will look for you is on the Internet. So obviously your website needs to be a digital representation of everything that's great about your small business. Not having a website isn't a choice. So where do you begin? It is all down to you, and how much you want to commit to building your own website. The choice is yours; do you build it yourself, or do you employ the services of web designers? There are pros and cons to both.

Build your own website

- You have control. Everything on the website is how you want it. From small things such as where the logo should fit, to more important and more complex operations such as how you might sell online.

- It can be cheaper. If you've explored how much that your website will cost, you realise that there's a huge amount of choice. To get a fully functional dynamic website, the cost is sometimes prohibitive. Therefore, if you build it yourself the cost will be much lower. Take into account the amount of hours that you need to put into it. If your business has nothing to do with digital technology, and you have no skills and experience, it might be better to get one built for you.

- You learn about the Internet and social media yourself, and you can exploit that new knowledge. We've used terms such as *smoke and mirrors* and *hot air* a few times during a discussion of digital marketing. One way to overcome this problem is to learn more about the Internet and social media by yourself. That way It is less likely that you will be exploited, and you'll have a less stressful time developing your online presence. Learning is an important part of your small business, and It is likely that you'll need to know the basics when discussing digital marketing with others.

- It takes more time, when you could be working on your business. The point is that your time is valuable, and if it is better spent doing other things, then you may have to buy-in digital talents.

Why not build your own website?

How to build your own website

In the following sections, advice is given on how to recruit a web designer to build your website on your behalf. Another option is to design and build a website yourself. One of the benefits of the Internet is that there are plenty of open-source, or free, resources for doing exactly that. It depends on how much time you have, and your level of interest. If you are short on time and you are not really interested in learning new technology skills, then it would be better for you to seek some professional advice. Let us take a look at some choices that you have; this summary is by no means conclusive, and you should investigate what works best for you.

Build your own WordPress site.

WordPress is free at the point of use software that you can use to create your own website. In a nutshell, the software for WordPress is being built by a community of volunteers; this means that there are a range of *plugins* that can be used to make your site unique, and to deliver a bespoke customer experience for your visitors. WordPress has more than 60,000,000 users. Most people that use WordPress are not web designers or IT specialists; they are novices.

There are thousands of free templates and themes for you to use, and the websites are easily customised. Whilst WordPress is often thought of as simply *a blog*, there are many other applications which can make it useful to your business such as the Content Management Systems (CMS) whereby large amounts of documents can be managed, galleries, ratings, shopping and ecommerce, video, and membership, as well as many other solutions.

A great place to start is on WordPress' own *showcase site*, https://wordpress.org/showcase/. There are plenty of interesting examples there, but realise that these are exemplars, and your own unique website will be as a result of your own hard work.

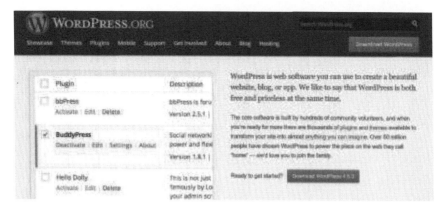

WordPress is both free and priceless

Organise a hosting account

You will need to pay for the services of a hosting company. There are plenty of them out there, and you'll probably only need to spend up to $10.00 or equivalent per month. Then you'll need to make sure that the web hosting company fulfils all of the necessary conditions for WordPress. This is a very simple process, as virtually all hosting companies have packages for WordPress. If in doubt, contact your hosting choice. Your will also need a domain name, www.your-company-name.com. Shop around, and do not always take the first price you are offered. Popular examples include Godaddy.com and Wix.com, amongst thousands of others.

WordPress' simple, 5-minute install

WordPress has its *Famous 5-minute Install*. If you are comfortable to run a basic installation, you will find this straightforward. Otherwise, consider using WordPress's more detailed installation instructions. Essentially, you will need to download and unzip the WordPress package. Then you will create a database for WordPress on your hosting account (web server), and you will also have to create a MySQL user account. Then you upload the WordPress files to your hosting account. Finally, you access your URL (http://example.com/blog/) and run the installation script by following the simple on-screen instructions.

WordPress is FREE! And it has loads of functions.

Once installed, WordPress is largely a WYSISYG (What-You-See-Is-What-You-Get) editor.

- You can easily add your logo, change the colour of the background, add some sliders to contain your images, and many other functions - without knowing a single word of code.
- There are more than 2700 WordPress themes. Themes are the skins of your website. They define structure and presentation; colour and fonts are also contained in your theme. Most themes are free, although some of the most professional and functional are paid-for; this is often the case as you develop your own website.
- You can decide upon which theme best suits your business, for example a sports theme, a transport theme or an ecommerce theme, amongst hundreds of others. The ecommerce theme might suit a hotel, a dress shop or a delicatessen. Spend time sourcing the best theme for you and your small business.
- There are more than 30,000 plugins. A plugin is simply an additional piece of software that seamlessly attaches itself to your website. It is like an app. This enables a degree of customisation for your site. Examples include SEO plugins, mailing lists, media players and post/page editors. As with anything which is open-source, read the recommendations first and note how many other webmasters have downloaded the plugin. Try to avoid anything with less than 4 stars and 1000 downloads.
- WordPress is designed to be friendly to search engines such as Google. SEO is straightforward with WordPress; it is developed using standard compliance, high quality code which makes your site irresistible to the search engines.
- The web site itself is really straightforward to manage. It is easy to update, and alerts you when a new version of WordPress is available. Plugins are updated in the same way. So, you can keep your website current and up to date.

- An example of this, is that WordPress now supports mobile devices and smart phones, including tablets. Simply by updating your WordPress Software one could add these new technologies to your standard website.
- A key benefit to the small business is that WordPress is generally thought of as being secure and safe. The Internet is an uncertain space, and there will always be intruders trying to help themselves to your website.
- WordPress now handles many different types of media. So, whilst you may begin your endeavours with text, you will have the opportunity to include images, audio and video content to enhance your user's experience. You can also embed Facebook, Twitter, Instagram and YouTube. As other social media and technologies develop, it is highly likely that you will be able to add these as the future unfolds.
- WordPress was originally designed to be a *blog*, which means that you can write content. Content is organised largely into posts which are the basis for your regular dialogue with your customers. You also have pages, which are your more standard web pages including your *contact page* and your *about us* page, amongst others. Posts tend to be far more numerous than pages.

Tip – back up your website

Back-up your WordPress site regularly. This can be done using a suitable plugin, although it is better to spend a fraction more and request a regular back-up from your hosting company. This will give you peace of mind.

Do you need something simpler?

Website builders, supplied by your hosting company.

If WordPress proves to be a little too demanding, then your next port of call should be a WYSIWYG (What-You-See-Is-What-You-Get) editor-based website supplied by your hosting company. This is far more user-friendly and there are far fewer opportunities for confusion and time wasting. There is also plenty of choice, and whilst such *Do-It-Yourself* websites are not free, they are relatively inexpensive in comparison to employing a web design company.

An example of a preloaded website builder - It is simple!

In common with WordPress, you do not need to know any code. The main difference is that you do not need to set up WordPress, since the DIY website is pre-loaded and comes with your hosting package. It is worth noting that WordPress also comes pre-loaded with some hosting packages, and this is another avenue for you to explore. However, the section will consider DIY website builders provided by hosting companies.

What are the benefits?

It is far simpler, and there is no opportunity to go wrong. There is often customer service support, and queries can largely be dealt with quickly.

The limitations are essentially that there is less functionality and the websites tend to be a lot less dynamic. DIY website builders are a good place to start if you are short on time, and want a quick and easy online presence. You can also anticipate that there will be many business themes included in the price of your package, that there will be plenty of space for your pages and images, and that there will be some mobile functionality too. You can expect to spend around $10.00 per month as you begin.

Some website builders will also come with an online store built in. This makes the package especially tempting, but may increase your monthly spend to as much as $50.00. This is a very straightforward way to begin selling your products online, although some packages may be more limited than others in terms of how attractive and engaging the product pages are.

Examples would include Godaddy.com in the USA, and 1and1.co.uk in the UK. There are many alternatives, and all major hosting companies offer a bespoke website builder in one form or another.

Start selling online. Your online store.

The most straightforward way to sell your products online is by using a hosted ecommerce platform. This means that you will have your own store with your own products; the hard work is done by the hosting company. In the same way as the DIY website builder, you build your store by making a series of choices. These stores are fairly rigid, whereby you can change colours, styles, content and Logos. This will be enough for many small start-up businesses. As your business grows you can invest in more complex online stores. There are a number of hosting companies which offer hosted ecommerce platforms. Let us consider two examples – Shopify and Yahoo Small Business Ecommerce (although there are many other alternatives available).

Shopify online store

Example. Shopify as a simple online store solution

Shopify is an example of a hosted ecommerce solution. It provides a wide range of professional themes, and a series of apps (similar to plugins for WordPress). It offers unlimited bandwidth, as well as unlimited products. It is really easy to integrate with shipping carriers, and has a mobile app for accepting payments and for managing your own store. There is also support from experts to help you get your store up and running.

Yahoo small business online store

Yahoo is simple, and looks professional

Yahoo Small Business Ecommerce is another popular choice. In fact, of all of the hosted shopping carts for small businesses, Yahoo has the greatest market share. Yahoo was one of the first companies to offer an online ecommerce solution to small companies, and therefore it has plenty of experience in the sorts of online stores that you may be setting up. The store itself is pretty basic, and it is possible that you will need something more elaborate. It does have plenty of options and you can integrate it with a number of payment providers, and transport options. It has stock/inventory control, as well as other useful features.

Get an Amazon Store

Think seriously about an Amazon store. Amazon is a very large marketplace for products. Unlike many of its peers, Amazon took the bold step to allow third party sellers to sell their products in its marketplace in return for fees. Not only will your products be exposed to a worldwide audience, but Amazon has extensive technology for selling and distributing goods in the current marketplace.

Take advantage of Amazon's exposure, technology and warehousing

Amazon is everywhere!

If you predict that you will be selling a larger number of products on Amazon, then it is best to go for their *pro account*. This also has the benefits of being able to load and track inventory in bulk, therefore there is a possibility that you will become a featured seller. Amazon prides itself on fabulous customer service, so as a third-party seller you need to focus on this too.

Deliveries will be fast.

For example, you will need to respond to all enquiries, good or bad, in 24 hours. Failing to do this not only results in a loss of sales and reputation, but penalties may also be imposed by Amazon. You'll need to make sure that you have a delivery carrier in place before you start trading; deliveries will be quite quick – Amazon Prime is a next-day service and it is becoming hugely popular. On some occasions 3 to 5 days is okay. Your carrier will need this flexibility. Speak to your carriers and explain your needs. They will have customers with similar requirements.

Aim for the Buy Box

Your aim is to get your product into Amazon's *Buy Box*. Almost 80 per cent of all sales are made through it. Amazon imposes a series of criteria to assess your company's readiness. For example, do you have strong feedback? Are your stock levels high, and is your price the best in the market?

Fulfilment by Amazon (FBA)

There is also the option to have order Fulfilment by Amazon (FBA). This is an additional service where products are shipped directly from Amazon's warehouse. Naturally this might cost a lot more, but the service could free up some of your time to do other work for your small business. Your orders will be picked and packed by Amazon, and returns will be dealt with by them. You need to balance the pros and cons before you make this decision. Another benefit is that you will be able to scale your business up fairly quickly because you do not have to purchase premises, or employ additional staff. Your customers will also have the opportunity to use Amazon's own delivery options, such as super-saver delivery and Prime. Therefore, it just makes the whole package more attractive to your customers.

Feedback must be excellent

Excellent feedback underpins your competitive advantage on Amazon. Therefore, it is really important that you ask your customers for their feedback, and it doesn't really matter whether the user experience was good or bad. If you have satisfied customers, give them an incentive to leave some good feedback. If you have dissatisfied customers, do your best to put things right and to impress your customer, then ask them for feedback.

Important: In the online world where products and services may be unfamiliar, potential customers use feedback to negate any doubts of fears they may have about the purchase.

Peer-to-peer (P2P) Ecommerce

Peer-to-Peer (P2P) ecommerce has many similarities to approaches already discussed. The main difference is that P2P is essentially based upon the marketplace where individuals sell to other individuals. Here we are going to look at some different opportunities for selling your products online within P2P environments.

Get on eBay

Historically, eBay was a place where individuals sold to individuals, largely to move possessions that people no longer required. Today individuals market goods on eBay as a profession; there are many small businesses trading successfully on eBay. eBay suggests a number of steps to consider before you start selling on their platform:

Do your research.

If you want to start selling garden supplies, find out how to ship them, had to wrap them, who your competition is, and other important marketing leg work. Earlier sections of this book give more detail on the specifics of finding out about competitors.

Your user ID.

Your online eBay name should depict what your business is trying to market, and reflect your brand. So, select something such as flowers4you, which reflects what you're trying to do and communicates with your potential customers.

Build up your feedback.

The company recommends a minimum of 25 positive pieces of feedback, with the ideal being in excess of 100 pieces. This means that you will need to focus strongly on, not only positive feedback, but also numerous feedback. The better you do here, the more realistic are your goals for success. Virtually nobody bids on sellers with no customer feedback -would you?

Develop your image and brand.

eBay recommends that you look to see how other successful sellers have developed their image online. Try to be as original as possible, and Do not copy. Work on your own brand, and your own personality.

eBay has professional sellers

Know your fees

Make sure that you know how much exactly you sell for; if you get this wrong by a few pence, then your losses may add up if you have a high turnover of products and low margins.

Know about your suppliers

Once again using research, make sure that you buy at a price that allows you a margin to sell profitably. It is not too difficult to buy wholesale, and make sure that you turn your stock over and make it liquid again. This will give you more money to invest in other products, and you do not want to be left with money tied up in stocks that you cannot sell.

Packing suppliers.

You need to give some thought to what packaging you are going to use to protect your product during its delivery. A useful tip here - that there are plenty of packaging power-sellers on eBay. You Do not want returns or dissatisfied customers. If in doubt, overpack.

Stock control.

It is difficult when you start out to work out how much stock you will need. However, you need to monitor and measure how much stock is sold in order to make sure that you replenish stocks once your sales start to increase. This is really important to eBay, because it does not want to see disappointed or dissatisfied customers. So, having gone to the effort of funnelling potential buyers to your product, it would be disappointing if there was no stock.

Selling tools.

Whilst you are selling a small number of products every week you will be able to control your sales. What happens if you start to become very successful? At this point your sales will be way beyond your personal control, and you will need to purchase software such as *Turbo Lister*, so that you are able to list items in bulk. Essentially the problem will be that you need to save time when listing the initial product, and software will save time.

Communication is the key to success.

Communicate with all of your buyers and sellers from the moment that they arrive on your page, make their initial purchase, when goods are shipped, and when they receive their items.

Also, communicate with them all the way through the bidding process, to the point where they are successful or otherwise. eBay will have no problems with you as long as you communicate clearly and politely with customers. They recognise that sometimes working with the public is tricky, and that no matter what you do some people will leave you with less impressive feedback. Just put it down to experience.

The Market-specific marketplaces

Is there a market-specific marketplace in your industry or sector? There is an emergence of *market specific marketplaces*, for particular industries. For example, in the arts and crafts space, there is a popular marketplace called Etsy. In common with eBay, Etsy is a peer to peer ecommerce website, with its competitive advantage focused upon handmade and vintage items. Products include toys, beauty products, jewellery, clothing and art, amongst other popular items. It also sells an extensive range of vintage products. As a small business person, you decide on the price of the item, so it is not an auction. Etsy simply takes 3.5% of the selling price. The initial set-up of your account is free, although each item is charged a commission of 20¢ and can remain on the website for up to four months.

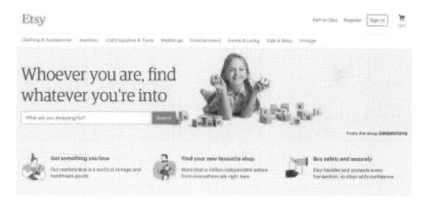

Esty is dominant in the arts, crafts and vintage markets

Look for smaller, emerging competitors

There are a number of competitors in the same marketplace as Etsy; including Aftcra, ArtFire, Bonanaza, Handmade at Amazon, Strorenvy, and Yakaboo. There are others as well. The point here is that once one major player emerges, smaller competitors start moving to the same market place. This is not just a case for arts and crafts products, other industries are also moving online in the same way and opportunities are opening up for other small business people to market their products online. You need to investigate your own industry and market, and find out the best ways to sell online through Etsy and its equivalents. As an entrepreneur, if you Do not find your online marketplace for your industry -perhaps you should create that site yourself!

Alibaba – the World's largest e-commerce company

Is Alibaba worth exploring? Alibaba is a Chinese e-commerce corporation which markets via its online web-portal. It is surprising how many small business people do not explore the opportunities that are presented by Alibaba. The business provides services for customer-to-customer (very much like eBay), business-to-consumer, and business-to-business organizations online. If this is totally new to you, then go to Alibaba.com and take a look for yourself.

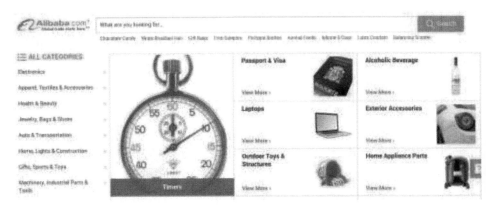

Take look at Alibaba.com. Is there an opportunity for your small business?

This fact might be surprising to you, but Alibaba claims that it is a more popular destination for online shopping than eBay and Amazon combined. Alibaba connects Chinese suppliers with buyers around the world for pretty much everything. It acts as an agent, or middleman, between suppliers and potential buyers anywhere in the world. There are many manufacturing companies in China that market themselves to mainly western, but also global clients. So, if you go to their website, then it is very easy to search for products, suppliers and even look for quotations from businesses largely in mainland China, but also from other nations including India and Brazil.

Alibaba example

Let us look at an example. You search for pianos. You are presented with an ordered list of 140,000+ items. There will be a minimum order quantity, and a pricing level. You import the products, and you make some money. Well maybe. Here is some advice.

When dealing via Alibaba, you might consider:

- You need to bear in mind that you are dealing with a whole array of different vendors. Therefore, you must take nothing for granted. You are dealing with the Chinese culture, and you need to investigate how to do business in China before committing yourself to anything. See later sections on *International Marketing* for more advice.

- Websites may not be up to date in China, so make sure that you confirm what you are actually buying and try to get samples if possible; otherwise ask the vendor to supply a recent photo.

- Most of the vendors are Chinese. Their level of written and spoken English is extremely good, in general.

- When ordering any item, you need to be very precise in what you say. Make sure you are absolutely clear about colour, the size, materials that the product is made from and packaging, amongst any other market specific need that you may have. Put this in writing, ask for samples, and ask for a photo of the product.

- Sometimes you may get something which you did not expect! Then you must be very assertive and demand that you get what you ordered. The more you sell, the more you will buy in the future and you must point this out to the vendor. Try to build a relationship with your suppliers.

- You can pay with PayPal, and a benefit is that you have some recourse if things are not as expected. You can use a bank wire transfer service, but once your money is gone - it is generally gone for good.
- A useful tip is to act bigger than you actually are. Obviously, you're a small business, although if you give the impression that you are larger than you actually are, then you are putting yourself in a better bargaining position.
- You can ask a series of questions to help you compare and contrast your potential suppliers. Ask them if you can have your logo put on to the products; try to find out lead times and minimum order quantities; ask them about quality and about how the product is made.
- Make sure that you are conforming to your local national laws – this is very important.
- Sometimes you will be dealing with trading companies, as opposed to the original manufacturer. Try to find out who the original manufacturer is. Sometimes trading companies will say they are manufacturers when they are not, and you need to be aware of this. Again, ask for photos of the factory.
- Once you purchase your product, you now have to get it from China to your own country. Most suppliers will say FOB, which means Free On Board. This means they will simply get the product to the local docks or Airport. You may then have a cost of transporting the goods to your own country. The weight of the products will affect transportation costs. The larger or heavier the item, the more it will cost to transport. Add to this the cost of local tariffs or duties in your own country, which are sometimes as high as 20 per cent! Also add any charges to get the products through customs and delivered to your own premises. The moral of this story is that the product may be cheaper, but once you get it to your premises the cost may be prohibitive. Check your figures carefully.

Globalsources.com is an alternative.

- There are other options too. Try *Globalsources.com* which is a competitor to Alibaba.

Buy in web designers. Invest in your online presence.

Of course, if you buy in any skills there is a price attached. Web design is no different. However, you must shop around, because hiring a web design company is going to be relatively more expensive.

With your own time, it is better to create a web design brief and then get some quotations. There are many web designers out there, and their skills vary as do their prices.

Write a brief based on your needs

You might decide to use a local web designer. This way if there is a problem, then you can make a phone call and pop over to see them.

Their reputation will be important to them locally, and if you have a poor experience you will tell other business people. They may be more expensive, so you need to take quotations.

Alternatively, you can source a web designer on the Internet. Again, proceed with caution. There are obviously some marvellous web designers who will connect with you online. It is the nature of their business. However, there are opportunities for more unscrupulous and less trustworthy individuals to offer services, which might cause you problems in the future.

Web Design Brief

There are some important elements that you might want to include in your web design brief. Let us have a look at some of them than here:

1. Tell the designer **about your business**. Explain what you do and tell them about your products or services. If you are a start-up or new business, then tell them this. Share with them some of your results from your background research into your customers and clients. Explain the sorts of social media that will need to be integrated to the website. Tell them about the sorts of promotions that retain customers. Remind them of your vision and tell them about your digital objectives. Explain what your competition is doing online.

2. Describe in some detail **what you want** from the website. Why do you need a website? Is it replacing a previous website? Show them a website from a competitor or from a different industry which you feel could be emulated. How many sections and sub-sections will your website need? Describe some of the key functions of the site – posts, pages, social media, membership and newsletters, any special forms, sections about you, and any maps. Will the website need ecommerce functionality?

3. Explain to the designer **about your visitors**. By talking about the individual traits of potential visitors, the

designer will have a better idea of how to make it more functional and customer focused. So, give them some segmentation information such as how old are your customers? Which country or locality are they from? What languages will they speak? Are you dealing with the general public or trade partners? Use marketing and competitor information from audits earlier in this book.

The designer will need to know why customers are visiting the website. Are they visiting to buy products? Are you entertaining the customers? Will visitors be looking for information? Are they looking for your contact details? Are they looking for videos? Are they looking for advice?

Finally, explain to the designer how much work **you intend to do**. Do you want to update the website yourself, and add new posts and pages? Alternatively, you may simply want to send an e-mail or make a phone call to get some changes made. Bear in mind if it is the latter, that the design company will charge you top dollar for even the smallest alteration. Our advice is that you will need to make some changes, and the website needs that functionality. Please see the section on WordPress, and similar sites.

4. What will the **final website look like**? You need to describe the look and feel of the final design of the site. It will need to reflect any corporate colours and Logos, and it must fit in with all of your other promotions and digital marketing. It must be integrated! Will the website have a traditional look or will it be more contemporary? Will it be a personal, blog style of website or does it need to be more professional?

5. Last but not least, **how much do you want to spend**, and when do you want to buy? Be very clear about your budget. It would be wrong for this book to tell you a

precise figure for your website. Speak to other entrepreneurs and small businessmen and ask them how much they spent. The rule of thumb here is, that if your gut feeling tells you that it is too much money - then it is too much money! Go away and shop around again.

Always ask for *examples of the web designer's previous work*. It is perfectly reasonable for you to contact the web designer's previous customers to ask them about their experience. You might even ask them how much they paid!

Once you decide upon your designer, pay them with a *series of stage payments*. Never pay them up front! If anything, pay them at the end. However, it is good to give the designer an incentive, so select a series of stages and agree the amount that you will pay for each stage.

Not happy? If there is anything that you do not like about the website, ask for it to be changed. Do not pay until it is changed. As with all of your suppliers, try to build a rapport with your web designer, keep him or her onside, and try to get the best out of him or her.

- Quicker because they already have the knowledge and software. If you want to hit the ground running, and you need a website building fairly quickly, then employing a web designer may be a better option.

More services from designers

Web design companies can often do all of your digital marketing. This is often the case in the modern digital world. However, be aware that you can sign up to too many digital options. Again, if in doubt, do not buy. There will be a series of services the designer will offer, so Let us take a look at some of them now:

Analytics and insight.

This terminology also includes **Search Engine Optimisation (SEO).** There is a section within this chapter on SEO, it is recommended that you read it before you buy any analytics and insight work. Essentially, SEO prepares your website for the search engines, and correctly will give you the best chance of ranking as high as possible within the search engines, such as Google and Bing.

Buyer beware! This is because some SEO specialists will promise all kinds of results, and tend to be relatively expensive. Often, they may recommend services that you do not actually need. It is also difficult for you to check their work; it is a little like taking your car in for a service and asking whether the oil has been changed; with little knowledge of how you can check.

Analytics and insight are discussed later in this chapter. Unless you have a website, which has a large amount of traffic, and or as a rule of thumb - is more than 100 unique visitors every day, it is not worth overspending on SEO. Of course, if you sell high value items, 10 visitors a day would make it worthwhile. Please see later sections on analytics.

Copywriting.

Copywriting skills are vital to any promotional campaign, and especially to digital communications. It is the *content* that is used in advertising and marketing. Copywriting will be used to write your website, to write any marketing emails, online advertising, but also in general copywriting is used for TV and radio scripts, press and media releases, catalogues, and sales letters.

Anywhere in your business where you use text or content, will need copywriting skills. Whether you buy them from your web design company is a matter for some thought. Of course, for your website and digital communications you might consider the designer; however, for a coherent and cohesive content message, you might do the copywriting yourself (based upon some of the material in this book), or you may employ a third-party copywriter to take on the whole responsibility.

Ecommerce.

Ecommerce it is essentially buying and selling online. To do this your website will need software to handle your products or services, and your customers and clients, payments and other features (as discussed earlier). The webdesigner should have the skills to write the code and set up the software for an efficient ecommerce website.

It is likely that the ecommerce infrastructure of your website is going to be the most expensive component. So, give this plenty of thought, and enter into discussion with your web designer about what is best for you. It is always worth doing a Google search, or looking on YouTube for some basic background advice.

Hosting.

Hosting is simply the place where your website is kept. It is basically a computer called a server. It is unlikely that your webdesigner will host your website on his or her business premises. There is plenty of third party space for hosting websites. This cost should not be too high for a small company. If you expect less than 1000 visitors per day, you can expect to pay less than $200 per annum for hosting services. If you pay more than this, you need to ask the question why? What are you getting in addition? For example, you might get additional backups of your website. This is a service worth paying for. If you need a very speedy site, you may pay more for this service. This is also the case if you have a large site of more than 1000 pages. If you have a very simple website, hosting should be really cheap.

Maintenance.

The website does not wear out! So, maintenance simply means updating your website. Although you may decide to do this yourself, or at least some of it. This is a basic costing exercise. Sometimes a web developer will charge you $100 to make small changes to a page.

So, if maintenance costs $500 per annum, and you want to make 20 changes during the year, then maintenance is a viable choice.

Beware when buying in web design services

But . . . Do they really know about your customers? Make sure that they have read the detail in your web design brief. If the webdesigner has not got a grasp of the needs of your clients, then they will not understand what is wanted from the website.

Are they simply changing a few things from other sites that they have built? This is quite a common problem with some more unscrupulous web designers. The actual framework and structure of websites can be copied and adapted, so that sometimes they are almost unrecognisable. Naturally there will be some common elements and software between almost all websites, especially WordPress. However, when you ask to see their previous work make sure that they are not simply recycling websites built for somebody else and charging you top dollar for their services.

Conclusion

Start your digital marketing as soon as possible. Make sure that you are not doing too much, and balance time with other business tasks. Decide whether to build your own website, or buy in talent to do it on your behalf. Set a budget and stick to it. If you are going to reach your market by retailing, eBay and Amazon need some careful consideration. Your digital offering will need to be monitored, and updated to keep pace with changes in technology.

Chapter 13 Search Engine Optimisation (SEO)

Most small businesses have less than 100 pages. This guide to SEO will focus upon the needs of small business and its website; if you have a large website or you specialise in ecommerce which depends upon a group of very targeted keywords, your need to invest more time and effort in SEO -or alternatively speak to your webdesigner about sourcing some specialist skills from elsewhere.

Perhaps more than anywhere in marketing, SEO is surrounded by smoke and mirrors. There are some unscrupulous SEO experts out there, so be careful. If in doubt do not commit. Here is why. Google, and all major search engines, will add your website to their index automatically. Make sure that you undertake some of the actions below; 100 pages will take a few days of your time. Keep it simple, and you will not need expert SEO help until your business is much larger. It will take time, and if you need instant results, consider Pay-Per-Click (PPC) such as Google AdWords.

So, the following will kick start any small business website.

SEO Terminology

SEO = Search Engine Optimisation

Domain = the name or URL of your website e.g. www.your-website.fr

URL = Unique Resource Identifier, means the same as domain (above)

Googlebot = software which Google uses to crawl your website, so that your content appears in the search engine result.

Google Analytics = is a free web analytics service offered by Google that tracks and reports website traffic.

Keywords = the main theme or topic of your webpage e.g. cheap+piano, budget+piano.

Crawl = Crawling is the process by which *Googlebot* discovers new and updated pages to be added to the Google index.

The basics of Search Engine Optimisation (SEO)

This section will give you the basics of Search Engine Optimisation (SEO). These pointers will give you the confidence to realise that your website is set up correctly without any obvious errors. It will signpost places for further information as well.

1. Would you prefer that your website visitors see WWW or non-WWW? Most small businesses keep WWW and so if you prefer this, then you need to do nothing. If, however, they you have a compelling brand name, you may decide that you want to get rid of WWW. If this is the case, you will need to add a 301 redirect. This is a simple piece of code that you add to your website so please Do not be put off. You can also add a plugin to WordPress, or you can ask your webdesigner to do this for you – for a small fee.

2. Sign up for Google Webmaster Tools. That this is a **free** service from Google. You will find it here: https://www.**google**.com/**webmasters/tools/** It would also be a good idea to select their free *e-mail forwarding* service so that you can receive any critical messages automatically from Google, such as if your site has been hacked or if it has become difficult for Google crawl it.

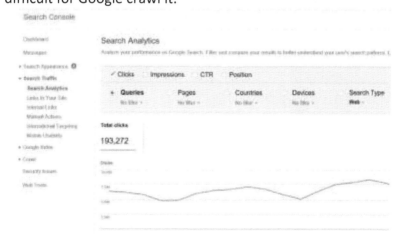

Google Webmaster tools are useful and free

3. It is a good idea to perform a background check on your website domain. The domain is your website's name e.g. www.your-business.com . This is because sometimes the website domain might have been owned by scammers. If this is the case then Google will penalise your website and it will not do well in the search engine. The way to do this is to do some basic online searches for your new or potential website domain. It will soon become clear if there was a problem with it. You can also look in your webmaster tools for any unrecognisable *keywords*.

4. The *fetch as 'googlebot'* feature is a really useful, especially if the site is new. You simply go to the feature in webmaster tools and paste your domain name into the dialogue box. You press enter, and the googlebot will crawl your website. This is one way that Google indexes all of the pages and content of your website.

5. Include your Google Analytics code. As you build a website for the first time, include your Google analytics code. This is the code that allows Google to collect data on your site which you can then use to improve your online strategy. There is more detail to support you with this in other sections. Again, this can be done with a simple plugin in WordPress; you can paste it into your webpage templates if you feel confident enough, or you can recruit the services of your developer.

6. As discussed in other sections, it is really important to make sure that your website best suits the needs of your potential visitors. This is your site design strategy, and it is contained in your web design brief. Google will automatically estimate how focused the site design is. It will consider how it meets the needs of each customer segment; it will also consider navigation and how easily users can get around your website; the search engine estimates how focused each page is based upon a logical theme or topic, so keep your pages focused upon specific *keywords*.

7. It is also a good habit to set goals. Google asks you to *define your conversion*. This is your Call to Action (CTA). So, having gone to the trouble of getting your potential customers to look at the web page, you do not want them to leave the page without having done something. So, potential CTAs would include:

    - Sharing your page using social media
    - Signing up to a free newsletter
    - Buying, or trialling your service or product
    - Entering a free competition
    - Downloading your free book
    - Signing up to become a member
    - Any other CTA which might be relevant to your particular industry or market

8. Make sure that you have *keywords* in your copy. Keywords are really important to Google and other search engines. Keywords are what your potential customer is looking for on your website; for example, if you sell fishing equipment, potential keywords would include rod, reel, and bait; if you sell legal services in Smallchester, then your keywords will be lawyer+smallchester.

Keywords should be focused

Use keywords that the average person would use to find you. Finally, in terms of your copy, try to answer some of the obvious questions that visitors to your website might ask; for example, how good is the product or service? Let users ranks and comment. Explain what customers should do if they are not satisfied. Include a satisfaction policy.

9. Every page and post should include some *unique elements* including:
   - Topic
   - Title (which is the part of the page which displays in the search results)
   - Meta description (which is the text which appears below the title in the search results)
   - Keywords in your filename, in lower case separated by hyphens e.g. www.cook-for-me.au/your-ideal-recipes
   - For each *link*, add a brief description known as *anchor text* (to both internal and external links) e.g. not <u>click here >></u> but <u>Your Ideal Recipes >></u>

10. Beware some obvious potential pitfalls. Try to avoid using a less reputable SEO company. Generally, if they promise the world they are unreliable. Never exchange or buy links. Indexable and searchable text should be prioritised over an elaborate design.

11. Speed is important. Try to make sure that your site's pages download in 2 seconds or less. Google aims for less than 0.5 seconds. You can test your website by typing in your domain name at Pingdom, here: https://tools.pingdom.com/

An example of Pingdom. How to measure the speed of your website and make improvements.

12. Ranking is going to be very important. Check it regularly. Google reasons that, to rank well, you need to provide an *awesome* product or service, that attracts *buzz*. Generate *+1s*, *likes*, *follows* and *shares*.

13. In terms of social media marketing, Google has a few tips:
    - Think holistically. Spread your message and identity to key social media sites, converse and discuss, and connect users to your pages.
    - Spend your time wherever your potential customers meet online or socially.

Conclusion

Much of your SEO can be undertaken by yourself. Google gives clear advice on what you need to do to rank well, which we have covered in this chapter. If you do decide to use SEO consultants, try to keep their services clear and focused. Ask them to tell you exactly what to expect and for how much. Get it in writing.

Chapter 14 Your social media

Social media will undoubtedly be a very important part of your digital marketing strategy for your small business. Again, as with many of the topics in this chapter, you may be expert or you may need to seek some assistance. If you use social media yourself then you are more likely to find social media marketing straightforward. However, as is often the case, some individuals simply prefer to retain their privacy and do not participate in any kind of social media activities. It is probable that you will be one or the other of these two types of person. So, in this section, the basics of social media will be explained before moving on to more technical approaches.

Social Media is vital

Again, clear and uncomplicated language will be used to describe the most useful features and benefits of social media to you, the entrepreneur or small business person. Social media communications fall under the banner of content marketing. So, before we investigate specific social media platforms, let us consider content marketing in general.

Content marketing

Content marketing is the management of content to engage visitors, followers and customers. Any medium which is on a webpage or social network can form the basis of content.

There are lots of examples of such tools and approaches; content may relate to material on social networks such as Facebook; it might be social streaming through iTunes or Spotify; content could be social publishing such as blogs or a personal website; it might be social knowledge such as Wikipedia; content media might include social searches such as Google Product Search; there are other examples such as social bookmarking sites including Reddit.

Social media content is king!

Therefore, content marketing controls text and video, and other tools such as games, aps, vouchers and so on, so that the visitor is engaged in communication and dialogue; this supports our longer-term relationship.

You will need to address a series of topics in readiness for content marketing.

- **Which platform** does our target market use to access content? Do they use traditional newspapers or magazines i.e. traditional print media? Do they use social networks such as Facebook? Do they use more than one platform to access content?
- How will they **participate with the content** which they access? Will they play games? Will they post messages? Will they circulate a viral e-mail?

- Can **content be syndicated**? Syndicated content can embed material from elsewhere on a webpage or in an app. RSS is an example of syndication.
- Which medium would be best to communicate with your **target group**? This often depends on whether the user accesses content via a tablet or laptop using Wi-Fi, or whether they are using mobile devices, accessing using 4G. Obviously the richness or size of downloaded video, images or text will vary depending on local download speeds; also think about target groups in international markets where speed is variable.
- Finally, what **actually engages** your target audience? What content will they actually value? Do they want video? Do they want to download maps? Do they want to pay with their phones or mobile devices? Do they simply need information in text format? Do they want to play games? Do they want to contact friends?

Facebook

Worldwide, there are over 1.65 billion monthly active Facebook users which is a 15 percent increase year over year. So, you can see that Facebook is an ideal avenue for you to communicate your messages, and so your products or services. Age 25 to 34, with 29.7% of users, is the most common age demographic. Therefore, if you are targeting the under 34 age group then you need to have a robust Facebook presence. Indeed, those aged over 34 are also likely to use Facebook in one form or another. However, as we reach the older age group of 70 plus, it is less likely that they will use Facebook or any form of social media. So, what do you need to get you going on Facebook?

Facebook is popular with most ages

The benefit of creating a hub for your business on Facebook is multifaceted.

- As Facebook puts it, it makes your **business discoverable** when people search for you on Facebook they will find you.
- It connects your business so that you can have **one-to-one conversations** with your customers, who might like your page, read your post and share them with their friends, and they can check on you every time they visit.
- Timing is also one of the benefits of Facebook as a social networking tool, since your page can help you reach large groups of people frequently. **Messages** can be specifically directed to their needs and interests.
- You can also **analyze your page** using insightful analytics tools, which give you a deeper understanding of your customers and how successful your marketing activities are.
- Facebook actually gives you a **web like address**, which you can put on your business cards, website and on your other marketing tools e.g. www.facebook.com/great-budget-pianos.

Get your business set up on Facebook

The starting point would be a Facebook company page. You need to do this to a good standard; otherwise potential customers may not take your business seriously.

1. You need to set up the Facebook profile. Go to www.facebook.com/pages and login. Click 'create page.'

Get your business onto Facebook

2. You are then presented with a series of choices, based upon what kind of business you have. Therefore, if you are a local business or place, you need to click on the icon for local business with place. Add details of your business, and click 'Get Started!'

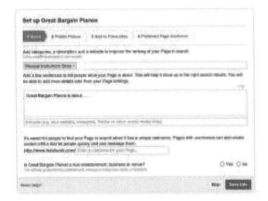

The sign-up process is easy

3. Complete the section about your company in some detail. Tell Facebook what categories you trade in. Finally confirm that your business is a real company. Essentially complete all other sections and finally click 'Save Info.'

Tell Facebook about your business

4. Next it will ask for a profile picture. Upload your company logo for an image of your product or service. Make sure that the image is high quality. A picture speaks 1000 words! You might decide to use your logo, or something else that represents your business, for example a picture of you or your idea, product or premises.

5. Adding your new Facebook site to *favourites* just makes it more easy to access. It is not absolutely necessary, it is just a matter of convenience for you.

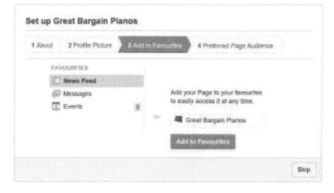

Record the page in your 'favourites'

6. The next page invites you to add some information about your business and your customers. This will help Facebook target your pages, in the same way that Google uses information to help its search engine to rank and prioritise. <u>Try not to get</u>

<u>drawn into any Facebook advertising programs; we are not</u>
<u>interested in advertising at this stage.</u>

Your business has a Facebook page.

7. Click through, and wow! Congratulations, and your small
    business now has its own Facebook page. The task now is to
    build your audience, start a conversation and develop some
    loyalty amongst your Facebook followers.

Building and developing your Facebook audience.

Once you have set up your company's Facebook page, now it is time to
build and develop your audience. Think about yourself as a user of
Facebook, and if you do not use it at the moment speak to friends or
relatives who are fans of Facebook.

It is good to sound out people in terms of the sorts of content and
communication that they would be interested in, and the types of
media that are most effective, and other issues such as how many
posts would be too many? Also remember that your social media is
part of an integrated approach to communicating with your
customers, and that the feel and look of all communications should be
in-keeping with your other media, such as websites and brochures.
Here are some tips to help you build and develop your Facebook
audience.

1. **How much is too much**? In your particular market, do people
    want to be communicated with once or twice a day or once or
    twice a month? If you run a small bistro, customers would be

interested in your lunch and evening meal menus, therefore twice a day would be ideal. However, if you manufacture musical instruments, twice a day would be too much. Therefore, once or twice a month would be much better.

2. **Facebook ads.** Okay, so when you start out with Facebook you are not going to have many followers. Therefore, a Facebook Advertising campaign may be something that interests you in order to get a critical mass of followers.

Very much like Google AdWords, you set your budget to a maximum and target specific groups of Facebook social media users. The process will seem familiar. Facebook will not run many ads on a page, and therefore if you have competitors which use Facebook too, you will enter a bidding competition for the best spots. So, go back and have a look at recommendations in terms of Google AdWords and how to get the most in terms of your budget, because the rules are very similar to those with Facebook ads.

You create your ad online, and then select the target audience. Then you specify your budget and use a calendar to schedule how you would prefer the adverts to run. Facebook has a trick whereby it bids on your behalf; bid yourself and make sure that you stick to your limits. The ads will continue to run until your budget has been used or until you reach the end of your schedule. You can extend your campaign, and you can also pause it.

What could go wrong with your Facebook campaign? This can mean that you are not getting any new leads and you are not selling any products and services.

- One of the major problems is targeting; this means that Facebook is placing the ads in front of the wrong audience.

- In contrast with Google AdWords, it is not such a good idea to direct your traffic from Facebook to your home page of your website or to a specific sales page for a product or service. The reason for this is that people using social media are not looking for products and services, in the way that they would by using the search engine. Their behaviour is different, because followers are looking to **socialise** with their friends. A better way is to try at trade off some knowledge or entertainment in return for a name and e-mail address.

- Returning to our pianos example, it is better to give away some video of the pianos being played by a celebrity or some piano music for beginners in return for a basic sign up. So, the landing page needs to ask for a name and email address.

- Test your ads for a low budget. Spend no more than $10.00 a day on testing your adverts, because this will give you all the information you need in order to assess whether the advert will be successful or not. If it is not successful end it; if it is successful, extend and develop it. Look for at least a 10% opt-in or conversion rate as a result of the advert.

- Make sure that the title in the advert is focused upon your target audience. You would use something along the lines of 'Are you looking for a cheap piano?' Adding some images may also make the advert more appealing. Again, test some of these out for a few dollars. In the description box make sure that you pack it with benefits for your potential customer.

- For a small business, it is especially important that you refresh your advert regularly. This may be every few days, rather than every few weeks. Change your title slightly, alter your image, and amend your description box. This may result in a slightly lower cost per click, so try it out.

- Another tip for a small businessperson, is to start broad with your target audience if you are a local business.

This means not limiting yourself by zip code, or by too narrow an age band. Start broad because this is likely to be much more cost effective and the ads will be cheaper to start off with.

3. Include your **Call-To-Action (CTA).** It amazing how many business people go to the trouble of setting up the campaign and then miss out their CTA! It has been mentioned before in this book. Do you want them to share something with their friends? Do you want them to click on the bottom? Do you want their opinions and views? Make it clear what you want people to do as a result of your Facebook marketing.

4. Get your **community** to answer questions and to offer tips and advice to each other.

5. **Competitions and contests** on Facebook. If your audience are engaging in your business and with each other, the competition will help you generate leads and extend their engagement. There are products such as Binkd and Strutta where you can set up contests for free, at first.

6. **Photos** of the standard currency for social media. Hence, they are very important for your Facebook page. Visuals create more interest and are quick and easy to digest.

7. The **timing** of your advert is important. If you have a restaurant, you may wish to promote your menu a couple of hours before people decide to go for lunch; you may decide to promote your Christmas meals two months before. Timing is important, and you must make sure that you are not too late, to take advantage of important social engagement.

8. A straightforward approach to early engagement is to ask your followers **questions**. Obviously if you ask them questions they are likely to respond, and this is the beginning of customer engagement with social media. They will also engage with each other. Make sure that your question is focused and polite

and not too controversial. The idea is that you want to engage a community in conversation, and retain them as customers.

Twitter

As with other social networks, Twitter takes its business pages seriously. Twitter can help you connect your business to what people are talking about at the moment. Twitter offers a social medium for people to talk about what they care about, as well as what is happening around them at the moment. This is a dialogue in which your business needs to be a main player. Twitter offers you a powerful medium to connect your message to what your customers are talking about in real-time.

Do your customers prefer to Tweet?

- You can listen and learn from what your competitors are tweeting or you can look for a list of industry keywords to help you gather intelligence. This gives you an insight into how you may adapt your social media strategy.

- As a medium social networks and Twitter are tools that will help you grow your business; you can run innovative promotions, develop your brand and have an engaging an ongoing dialogue with your customers (and you can use Twitter ads as part of your campaign)

You have 140 characters (although trials are being run with 280 characters) to get your point of view across; and your campaign can be innovative and maybe even viral. Let us take a look at how you set up your small business Twitter account, and then we will consider the best ways of engaging with your customers using Twitter.

Engaged with 140 characters.

To offer some praise to Twitter, the sign-up process for a small business is really straightforward. Its point by point structure advises you how to go through each step.

1. **Start** by going to this URL: https://business.Twitter.com/en/basics/create-a-Twitter-business-profile.html

2. Then continue by deciding what you want to use as your **Twitter username**, such as @bargainbudgetpianos, or @yourlocalbistro. Your username is also known as your handle (from citizen band radio). Make sure that the handle relates strongly to your business and you use your business name, if it is still available. You have up to 15 characters to do this. Twitter is all about short and succinct messages, and you'll get used to this.

3. You can add a **profile photograph**. Take a picture of your business or use your logo. Also, please remember that it will not only appear on your logo page, but also next to your name whenever you Tweet.

4. You can add a bio, or **biography**. This is where you write about your business and explain why it is different to any other. You have 160 characters to do this. This is where you can put your precise information such as your opening hours, a link to your website and directions to your location. If you have a special landing page or social media, as is recommended in the Facebook section, add a Call To Action, and grab your visitor's name and e-mail address. As discussed, this is a social interaction and people will only go to your website if they feel there is something which adds value to their day. So, give away some free information, media or a product or service. Never forget your CTA.

5. For your small business, you can add to your **header image** which is a banner or billboard for your company. You can make this the cornerstone of any promotions and you can refresh it regularly to keep your customers engaged.

6. Finally, you can add a **pinned Tweet**. Put simply, this means that you can pin a Tweet to the top of your timeline so that it remains in the same place all the time. This is ideal for some current information that you need your clients to see when they visit your Twitter page. The pinned Tweet can be a promotion or some latest news, or anything else which they might find interesting.

Building and developing your Twitter audience.

Twitter is essentially a series of very short and punchy announcements, or comments, about what members are doing at a particular time. There is no opportunity to engage your customers with the reply option, and the community can see what each other has said. As the number of followers, you gain grows, then you are entering into a dialogue with your customers. Twitter happens in real time, and it is live 24 hours a day - so not everybody will catch what you're saying all of the time.

Your point in 140 characters

Remember you only have 140 characters (which include any gaps) to say what you want to get over to your customers. Be clear, succinct and brief. Try not to keep saying the same thing and keep your messages fresh.

Twitter isn't for selling things! So as with other forms of social media, you need to drive your audience to a page which grabs their name and e-mail address, so that you can market to them in the future. Offer nuggets of information or some freebies to get them to click through your CTA, and to sign up. Expect the better Tweets to be retweeted, that means they get shared and passed along, and commented upon, by other Twitter users. In today's digital market, customers are far more likely to buy from companies that have a proactive Twitter account.

Here are some tips to help you build and develop your Twitter audience.

1. In the early days of your Twittering, you need to make sure that it is a priority and that you **tweet regularly for a few months**. Generally, those businesses that have tweeted more than 10,000 times have far more followers. So, make it an unbridled passion, and become addicted to Twitter in the short term. There are lots of benefits this, since you will write sharper and more focused Tweets, become more comfortable using Twitter signs and symbols, and will focus and target your content to the ear of your followers.

2. Go to your other social media, such as Facebook and especially LinkedIn, and to your e-mail database and attempt to **recruit new Twitter followers**. For example, if you go to your LinkedIn context page and select settings, you will have the option to export all of your contacts to a .CSV file – add this to your e-mail database. Then from your Twitter account you can upload your e-mail contacts/database and select which ones you want to follow.

3. Having developed your Twitter audience, you need to ensure you **tweet on a regular basis**, so that your followers retain their interest in your product or service.

4. Tweet when you have a small amount of spare time, for example when you are on a bus or train, or when you are taking a break in a café. These **small moments** are productive when it comes to social media.

5. Become an **expert in your field**. This is true with much social media, but especially so with Twitter. Whilst the word expert is sometimes a debateable term, followers will expect you to be knowledgeable about your subject and will refer to you for guidance and information. The idea is that you elevate yourself to the level of expert and fulfil your claim. Always remember the **importance of integrity**, and if you offer poor advice your level of expertise will be questioned.

6. **Ask them questions**, and engage with your Twitter followers. This has the benefit of perpetuating the conversation, and it has a degree of longevity to it as well.

7. You will become a **curator of good content**. On your travels around Facebook and Twitter and other social media, retweet anything that you think your followers will find valuable and will support your position of expert.

8. **Twitter is not a selling opportunity**. It is a social community. Use it to network people and only promote your goods and services, from time to time. You will see other Twitter users making this mistake often, so try and avoid over-selling.

9. Always **be polite** and friendly, and never engage in anything controversial.

10. If people follow you have a look for something interesting, then return the favour by **following them back**.

11. Always make sure that there are **links** back to your website, and to your other forms of social media.

12. Make sure that you have your icon, or your photo **displayed prominently** in your Twitter profile.

13. Your Twitter profile must always **be complete**. Make sure that you have not left any gaps in your profile.

LinkedIn

LinkedIn company pages allow you to showcase your business and to target your audience; you may even have personal pages for yourself or for your small business. Initially you would create a company page by entering your name and company e-mail address – it is that simple. Then you simply verify that you are eligible to create a page on your company's behalf. You create a company profile by offering a company description and overview; this needs to be quite short and salient and it needs to show what your business does, why it is different and what it specialises in.

Build your small business based upon networks, collaboration and expertise

You would then add a banner and your logo to tailor the LinkedIn company page with your own branding; the logo will appear when other LinkedIn members search for your small business and it will appear on your employees' profiles, should you have any at this point.

You can add your company profile to other marketing channels such as websites, e-mails and newsletters – as you can with all your social media.

Building and developing your LinkedIn audience.

Followers are your influencers and your customers, and LinkedIn will encourage you to invest time and resources to establish a robust follower base. Then, as with other social networking tools, you need to devise rich content to share with your followers; this means that you are beginning your dialogue. For example, by posting company updates you start your conversation and word of mouth marketing begins to develop engagement; you can check company news, articles and even hot topics.

LinkedIn in three steps

LinkedIn recommend that you promote your small business online based upon three steps. Step one is **profile**, step two is **network** and step three is **relationships**. Let us take a look at these briefly, and other ways in which you can exploit LinkedIn for your small business.

Step one is profile.

- You need to **understand your audience**. This is something which you may have done for Facebook and for Twitter, for your website and for other social media. It is back to targeting segments of customers and engaging with them with useful and compelling content. This theme is firmly embedded in this chapter and throughout other parts of this book.
- Organize a **professional photo**. This is really important. Find a recommended professional to take your photos. Ask for samples of work and make sure that you do not spend too much. A ballpark figure would be about $300 in the first instance. You're putting a face to your name and first impressions are really important. A decent profile photo will give you far more connection requests.

- You have the opportunity to **create your own headline**. This will support your photograph and will be the first things that your LinkedIn viewers will see. Include some keywords that your visitors might be looking for, such as pianist or trainer. This will make it appear higher in the searches on LinkedIn for areas of your own expertise.

- You have an opportunity to **provide a narrative**. A narrative is a story about yourself and how you arrived at your particular role, at this point in time. For your small business, you can tell the story of how it all started and what you want in the future.

- Customers will be really interested in this, as well as collaborators and networkers.

- You have the chance to use LinkedIn to **showcase your work**. By giving examples, you will be able to gather more interest and allow people looking at your profile to get a better idea of what you do. You can include things like images, and websites, and any presentations which you have done.

- **Recommendations and endorsements** will let your network speak for itself. It is really easy to let these opportunities go by! So, you need to seize the moment. If somebody e-mails you with thanks or comes up to you and praises you in some way, obviously thank them in return - and it may be a good idea to ask them for a recommendation. Sometimes you can exchange recommendations, and write one for them in return.

- Do not hide yourself! By over complicating things, sometimes you can make yourself difficult to find. Therefore, **make yourself easy to find**. For example, go to the Google search engine and look for yourself. If your LinkedIn profile is high, perhaps one or two, then you have got this right. If not, go back and refine your LinkedIn profile to make it more straightforward and easier to find.

- **Business networking** is the name of the game for LinkedIn. This is its competitive advantage. The first step is to create your **core connections**, who are the people that you intend to converse with on a regular basis and who will be the foundation of your professional network. Your initial network will be friends, family, colleagues and clients with whom you already have a relationship. These are the people that will say great things about you. LinkedIn will go through your address book in your e-mail account, and ask you if you want to add people. This may save time, but make sure that you are selecting people who want to network with you as well.

Use LinkedIn for business networking.

- You can also network with **classmates and alumni** from school and university. Look for people that you worked with and customers that favoured you in previous job roles.

- LinkedIn has a feature called **Groups**. Groups is a place where you can meet like-minded individuals; it is the equivalent of Google+ communities, and Facebook groups. Naturally, the difference is that these are always professional groups; for example, if you are a member of a professional institute they will have a LinkedIn Group, or if you spend time working for a large well-known brand – it too will have a LinkedIn Group in all probability.

- With social professional networking, you need to make **connecting with people part of your daily business routine**. So where as in the past you would have exchanged business cards, or jotted down telephone numbers on a piece of paper, now you will link in with people that you meet at business events or any kind of networking occasion. This needs to become a habit. The idea is that whilst you may not want to do business with these people now, in the future you may have a need to network or collaborate with them.

- You can gain **new contacts** by *reaching out* to LinkedIn members. This entails looking for a mutual connection you are to contact or somebody that you might want to be introduced to; this is called an *introduction*.

- The way that LinkedIn makes its revenue is as follows. If you do not have an initial contact with a suitable connection, you have to pay for **LinkedIn's Premium service**, which is called *InMail*. Use **InMail** only if it generates a contact which can lead to a new customer, or ultimately may increase your income. There is a cost to InMail, so look for benefits in return – otherwise use their FREE services.

Step Three is Relationships

- Now that you have a critical mass of contacts on LinkedIn, it is time to start doing something with them. This is what we call **relationship building**. It takes a lot of resource and effort in order to build relationships, and it will take time. The outcome should be a valuable contact who you might collaborate with in the future, in order that your small business grows in one way or another.

- The term **expert** is used again. You need to demonstrate that you are an expert in a particular field and you can do this by sharing your interests, any news you might have and videos too, should you have the commitment and time to create them.

- LinkedIn argues that you can become a **thought-leader** by posting on LinkedIn. Posting on LinkedIn must be saved for relevant and value based content. It is very much like timeline on Facebook, although it is not for conversational discussion, but more for professional engagement with like-minded individuals.

- Smartphones are essential to all social media, and LinkedIn has a **LinkedIn Connected app**. It now includes the anniversaries of job changes and promotions. Again, if it is not useful, do not spend time on it.

- **Reminders** are a useful tool to use on LinkedIn. You can remind yourself to get in touch with a contact, or series of contacts, on a regular basis. You would simply go to the profile of the individual in question, and set a reminder – It is really simple. The argument is that you need to nurture and develop valuable relationships with certain individuals.

- **Who has viewed your profile?** Is a feature on LinkedIn (but you have to pay for it if you want to see all views). The idea is that you can see if the content is driving people to view your profile; you can see who is viewing it directly after reading a particular post. This gives you the opportunity to tailor messages for specific groups, and gives you a ballpark measure of success.

Google +

Google + is Google's main social media offering. It is a very powerful tool for social networking, but it has more to it than Facebook and Twitter, since it links together all of Google's services for a unique experience. Hence the next section on YouTube is closely aligned to this discussion since Google owns YouTube. Although, let us face it, Google+ has struggled in the face of strong competition from Facebook, Twitter and Instagram (now part of Facebook). It is a truly excellent tool, and it is free! However, others social media companies have 'land grabbed' social media users. To its advantage you can integrate Google maps, Google reviews, and it also will appear in the Google search engine should your small business be searched for specifically.

Google + is a collection of business services

So, there are pages specifically designed for businesses on Google +. Here are simple series of steps to get you going;

- You choose an accessible **Gmail account** for your business, then you create your own page using your Gmail account. You are able to select your business location, discuss your products or brands, explain about your company as an organisation, and there are other things that you can leave information about. You are effectively signing up for a regular business account, rather than a small business account.

Your start-up on Google. Hello World!

- You need to **customise** your public profile. You can include your tagline and an image or logo. Then as with other types of social media, you can promote your page by creating a series of networked circles.
- Finally, you launch your page and measure and adapt your social media strategy.

Building and developing your Google+ audience.

1. As with other flavours of social media, first of all you need to **create a personal profile**, in addition to your business page. As a small businessperson, this will reinforce your own personal brand. This is an option in Google+, whereby you can merge the two accounts. Naturally, if you do not wish your personal information to become public, then stick to your logo and your business's own brand. Conversely, if you are the central driver of your business, and you have used your personal image in other forms of social media which support your idea, start-up or small business, then do not confuse matters by having two accounts. It is an option here.

2. In contrast to Facebook's timeline, Google+ has more of a **personal mini-blog**. Therefore, you can write pieces of content that your followers would be interested in which would certainly be longer than any Twitter post (tweet), but gives the opportunity to write more extensively than Facebook. You need to write posts which add-value and retain interest. Therefore, your Google + page needs to be updated often, and in some ways, it is like a personal website too. So, it is safe to say that Google plus has moved into a space somewhere between Facebook and personal blogging.

3. Google+ offers the option of **creating your own circles**. A circle is a cluster or group of friends with particular interests, or in other words a segment. Follow other potential customers or collaborators who have similar interest to you, in the hope that they will follow too, and you can add them to your circles. In addition, follow religiously those circle members or followers whom you are most closely related to, so that you can build up

a critical mass of interest with other opinion leaders and potential customers. Obviously, you cannot do this with all of your followers – but select a few relevant ones, and concentrate posts, and responses, on them.

4. Another niche service offered by Google for social media, is its **trending report** which is updated in real time. This means you can spot topics which are hot at the moment and join in with a discussion, introducing your expert skills and sharing them with your community and others.

Spot what's trending and join the curve

5. One way of connecting with other users is simply to use Google's **search function** in order to find your target audience. You can use Google's *Ripples* feature to see who is worth listening to and investing time in. Essentially the *Ripples* feature summarises the popularity of particular posts by individuals, and considers how much they had been shared.

6. Google has many innovative ideas, which it has integrated into its Google+ product. One such concept is the idea of a **Hangout.** A hangout is a good way to add-value to your business or add yourself as a personal expert. They are a live way to broadcast to the world for nothing. It is like having your own TV channel! They take a lot of time to plan and to implement, and they will take some commitment on your part. Nevertheless, it is a concept which is untested and therefore who knows how popular it will be?

7. Google+ has a really interesting feature whereby you can **create events** and invite your friends. The idea is that you create a circle of your Google+ followers, then you create an

event for your hangout and send an invitation to everybody within that circle. Obviously use your marketing and copywriting skills to deliver a compelling title and banner to entice people in. Encourage people in your circle to share the event with other people too, targeting them or a similar kind of individual.

8. Google is very fond of getting us to link to topics, as a way of voting for what we like. It is the same here with Google plus, and there are a series of tricks to get people to link to your material. Let us have a look quickly at a few:

   - mention other users in your post - and hopefully they will mention you in theirs too;
   - use a #hashtag to link your posts to relevant topics, such as #playbargainpianos.
   - You could go through trending topics and link to some of them, and persuade your users to +1 your posts, which is exactly the same as Facebook share;
   - invite your friends and followers to like your business.

9. Google has a really useful feature called **communities**. These Google+ communities are forums or message boards, and are very similar to Facebook groups. Essentially you are trying to join the people with similar interests together; on the other hand, you could join a series of relevant communities in order to promote your own personal brand, and to gain more followers.
10. Finally, add the Google+ badge to your website.

YouTube Channels

YouTube channels give your business the opportunity to record and publicise videos. It is worth noting that YouTube is part of Google. It might be advisable at this stage to use the same Gmail account as you did for Google +; it is likely that Google will automatically integrate the accounts, so trying to keep them separate is probably pointless. The medium gives you the opportunity to network with more than 1 billion+ people worldwide who visit YouTube monthly. So, you need to ask yourself what you want to get from YouTube and integrate it into your marketing digital marketing approach.

YouTube has an audience more than 1bn

- set yourself **goals** in relation to what you want the channel to achieve. This is likely to be in terms of how many times the videos and watched, and by whom.
- decide on how best to **adapt** the you Tube channel to suit your corporate identity; for example, you can customise channel background and add logos, and details about your organisation.
- you may need **commercial software** products such as *Camtasia or Sony Vegas* (or one of many other options) to record your videos. You can often get a 30-day free trial, so you can create your first videos for nothing – then buy the software once you are used to it. Of course, you could bring in a professional video company to produce your videos on your behalf. However, it is anticipated that most small business people will need to do much of this by themselves. Therefore, learning to use these types of software will help you to make videos more quickly, with a professional style.

You'll need some basic software to edit videos in readiness for YouTube.

- **other tools** will include *microphones and video cameras*. Let us face it, if you have a decent smartphone, it will do the job. However, to extend a point made earlier about your profile picture on social media, you need to generate a professional persona for yourself; therefore, invest in a high definition camera, and a decent microphone. Be prepared to spend $300 to $500 on these items (although you could easily spend more!).

- once the video is uploaded, think carefully about how you **describe the video** and the tags you use; they need to appeal to your target audience.

- you can **organise your video content** as *individual videos* or *playlists* based on particular topics or themes; again, think about how your users will want to access the videos.

- you will probably want to **allow comments** on your YouTube videos, and if so you will need to make sure that your business is *checking comments regularly* and that it feeds back on all comments as quickly as possible; it is all part of the global dialogue with users. If comments cannot be managed, then switch them off, although viral marketing needs comments to fuel the fire.

- as with other forms of social media you can **promote them** on your website or through any other channels which you use regularly, or you could use Google AdWords or similar PPC solutions. Promote your videos through your social media channels such as Facebook, LinkedIn, Twitter, Google+, and Instagram, as well as others that you may use.

- YouTube has very **detailed Analytics**, so you can measure reactions to any changes you might make to your social media campaign. It is also a good idea to include your YouTube channel within your Google analytics data.

Building and developing your YouTube audience.

YouTube has more than one billion of users every day. Viewers watch hundreds of millions of hours of videos, and generate billions of views. Growth of YouTube has accelerated by at least 50 per cent year on year over the last few years.

So, you have decided to use by YouTube as a medium to communicate with your audience, and to recruit and retain some new customers. Let us look at some tips and tricks that will make your YouTube experience more comfortable.

You video equipment

1. Today, quality videos are easier to produce than ever before. Yes, they are going to take some practice, but that's fine. If you follow vloggers (video bloggers) or business people online, you will see that over time their videos improve, not only in quality but also in content.

   You'll also see that the presenter or commentator gains in confidence as time progresses. Everybody is nervous at first, but you need to give it a go. If you Do not like the videos, you can change them or you can delete them.

To get started you need a microphone, a camera and some lighting. As mentioned previously you can use your current smartphone or invest in an HD video camera; up to $100 on a reasonable microphone would be an investment; some lighting might increase your expenses by another $200, but this will improve the user experience tremendously. You might also spend another $100 on an animated introduction or exit from your videos. There are plenty of online creatives who will happily help you with this.

Tips and tricks for video

2. If you have read the other sections on social media, you will be beginning to spot obvious patterns in digital marketing. YouTube has similarities to Facebook, Twitter and other social media platforms. However, YouTube is a video medium, and there are some tricks that you can use that might not be employed in other types of social media.

- **Grab attention in the first few seconds**. If you Do not do this, your visitors will stop your video and look elsewhere. Try to ask a question at the beginning. Introduce something compelling in the video to grab attention, such as the location where you film the video.

- **Keep it short and simple!** The most entertaining and compulsive videos are generally quite short, i.e. between 1 and 3 minutes. You can use your *attention score* on YouTube which will tell you where in the video people tend to drop off or leave. If they leave a 10-minute video after 4 minutes, then you know your video is too long.

- **Tell a story.** An essential inclusion is a narrative. Without a story, there is nothing compelling for the viewer to watch.

Be informative

3. Rather than vlogging, perhaps your videos are more likely to be *informative*, i.e. your telling your audience about your products

and services. This needs a slightly different approach. You might develop a tutorial on how to do something, for example how to play a simple tune on a piano.

This could then develop into a series of different tutorials, and you can use them as a way to showcase the pianos that your selling in your online store. These steps will give your viewers a systematic series of tasks to accomplish, and is a good way to showcase your business in a positive light.

The attention scores will be interesting here; you might notice a high drop off very early on, but then those people that watch a whole video will remain to the end and the attention score will be relatively high. Showcasing videos can be much longer than simple vlogging videos; this is because people are gaining knowledge and insight and are prepared to invest more time.

Annotations

4. Introduce some *annotations* into your videos, such as a CTA, Call-To-Action

Plan your videos

5. One important recommendation is to **plan your videos**. Here are some simple steps to help you structure your YouTube production planning:

- **Research your keyword.** Google has a keyword tool which will show you what is popular at the moment, and what is not. Try to find keywords which are less competitive, giving you the chance to rank higher within a YouTube search.
- If you have used **a transcript**, then once your video is completed it is a good idea to upload it to YouTube. It will help Google to direct suitable traffic towards your video.
- If you have put time and effort into other social media platforms, such as Facebook, make sure that you are **cross-posting your videos**. This cross fertilisation between your

social media platforms is really important, and something which we will explore later in this chapter in more detail.

- If you have a blog or website, then **embed your video** within it and share it.
- If you have an **e-mailing list**, prepare an e-mail to tell your readers about the videos

6. In YouTube, you can add a **featured channel**, which is almost like your own television channel. Again, use marketing techniques to develop and promote it.

7. **Add to your videos regularly**, and block out time in your calendar to do them. Another technique is to spend a few days doing nothing but filming videos. Then post them at regular intervals. This means that you do not have to reacquaint yourself with your equipment every time you want to film a video.

Instagram

What is Instagram?

Instagram is a mobile photo sharing application, whereby you can share photos, videos and a number of other social networking services. It involves far less commitment than Facebook, and in some ways, is the pictorial or visual version of Twitter, in that it is short and sharp.

Images can be shared either privately or publicly as well as through the usual social network platforms of Facebook and Twitter, as well as others.

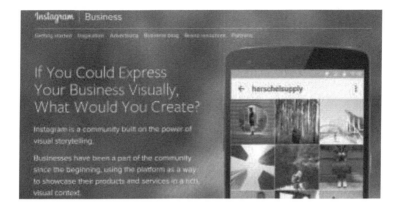

Instagram is great if your business is visually innovative or attractive.

Download the app

Instagram can be downloaded from an app store, and you should login using your Facebook profile or your e-mail account. From here, you get taken to your news page which is a summary of recent images supplied by people that you follow. You can flick through these images, and double-tap them to like them, or you can leave a comment. If you want to see more from a particular person's posts, you can click on their profile and look at other recent images.

Instagram terms

You may come across the term #, or hashtag. Posters will use the term #hashtag, to label their images so they can be found through global searches. So, if you're a selling bargain pianos, you might use #fabulousbargainpianos. If your business has a particular name or event, then hashtag might be a useful way of promoting it.

Start getting Instagram contacts

You can search for a particular person by using their username. There is a list of people that are following you, or that have recently commented or liked your posts. You can choose to follow some of them back. Make sure that in your settings, you include a link back to your main website. Also ensure that your business is named correctly. As with Twitter, you can follow other people. You can automatically follow people who are Facebook friends, or import a contacts list from your phone or other social media. You can set how you share your images with other people, so that they automatically appear in other social media.

Compelling images

If you are using Instagram for business, it is important that your images are interesting to your followers and are compelling in some way. As with all other social media, you are telling a story about your business and your brand and you want it to look as clear and professional as possible.

You can import images from your smartphone, or you can take a picture in the moment, and instantaneously upload it. There is also the option to record and upload a video. The Instagram Software allows you to edit your photos, and use other features such as filters. As you upload to Instagram, you are encouraged to write a brief but interesting caption. The **caption** is almost like your CTA in that it grabs attention. As with other forms of social media, you can **tag** someone else in the photo if they appear. You can also set the **location** where the image was taken, which is important if you have a location-based business. Finally, highlight those other forms of social media which you intend to share your image on. Then click share and it is all done automatically!

Building and developing your Instagram audience.

Let us take a look at how you can use Instagram to market your business digitally.

1. Only post images based upon topics which will be of **interest to your audience**.

2. Instagram should be **consistent** with all other forms of social media. So, make sure you use the same branding, logos, and themes in your images.

3. You must make sure that you have gone into settings and **connected Instagram** with your other forms of social media. Make your images public.

4. **Measure your likes**, and look to see what is successful. Consider which images are commanding more likes (that is the little *heart-shaped* button), and ask yourself why? Is it because it has pictures of your products? Is it because of the colour or background? Is it because it features people? Ask yourself why some more popular than others, and try out different techniques to get more likes.

5. Encourage followers to **upload their images** too! You do not have to be the only person that uploads images of your products or services. One way of doing this is to have a competition to see how many shares for likes an image can get, based upon a product or service which is supplied. This is becoming more and more popular, so you must make sure that your competition idea is different in order to grab the enthusiasm of participants.

6. You should always **respond to any comments**. This is good practice for all your social media. Good or bad, you must always handle any feedback via social media. In fact, if you deal with it positively it shows your business in a good light.

7. Do not forget your **#hashtags**; as a small business, your images will be made public, and the # makes it easier for your images to be found in a search on Instagram.

8. Consider using **videos**; they do not have to be too professional since people might not expect too much from an Instagram video. If you are a café you could show your food being made ready for today's lunch menu; if you are selling pianos, you could play a brief tune which is a demonstration.

Pinterest

What is Pinterest?

Pinterest is a social media tool which encourages its users to share visually, and to discover new interests. This activity is known as *pinning*. You effectively create digital notice boards which are a collection of pins which have a common theme. You can keep a set of notice boards yourself, you can share them, and you can look at what other people are pinning too.

Some would reason that Pinterest is essentially a bookmarking site. Pinterest is very visual; in the past one needed an invitation to join, but now you simply sign up. It is free, and certainly warrants some investigation on the part of the small business or start-up.

Pinterest is a digital notice board

You can sign up as an individual, or as a business. Obviously if you have promoted yourself as an expert using other social media, you will want to sign up as an individual; however, if you are promoting your brand or a location-based business you may prefer to sign up as a business. So, let us look at some tips on how to promote your small business using Pinterest.

- make sure your **pin categories** relate strongly to your target groups.

- ensure that your **profile is complete** including a full background to your business, and a professional photograph or logo.
- certainly, in the short term, you can use **pinalerts** which will send you an e-mail every time that somebody pins something from your website.
- it is really important that you **respond** to any comments or questions about your pins.
- your boards will look fuller if you have about **10 images** on them. The fuller the boards are more attractive to followers.
- add Pinterest **follow button** to your website, or even a Pinterest profile widget.
- **re-pin** your customers' Pinterest boards. This shows that you have taken an interest in your followers.
- if you write articles for your blog, or you have a newsletter for your website, make sure that you pin these **articles** on to a board.
- as with other social media, make sure that you are **targeting** the right customers with the right message. Do not try to lead somebody to a sale immediately. Try to get some information from them and retain them as a follower, before you try any marketing of products and services to them.
- in common with many other social media companies, Pinterest now generate income via advertising which it calls **promoted pins**. Essentially it does exactly that; you increase your click-throughs and your reach, and potentially increase traffic to your website too. This is a Pay-Per-Click (PPC) service.

Social Media Management Tools

You may wish to coordinate the usage of your social media approaches, and for this you need a social media management tool. Let us face it, if you have a lot of social media to control, and you may even have more than one the website or persona, then how can you effectively and efficiently co-ordinate such a task? Well, you would use a social media management tool – and there are plenty of them.

What are social media management tools?

Social media management tools allow you to connect all of your different types of social media, such as Facebook, Twitter, Pinterest, Instagram and others. You can schedule an entire campaign so that your social media communications are dripped out over a period of time.

As a small business person, you need to be aware that some of the services are free and others are charged for. Also take into account that some of the free providers may become chargeable in the future. It is best to assess your needs for today and in the near future, and look for a cost effective alternative. If you are going to use a lot of social media for your business, then consider investing in some of the more advanced tools, software or dashboards. The next section will consider a few of the most popular tools.

Hootsuite

Hootsuite is by far the most popular tool for most social media management. It is used by many businesses to deliver campaigns across many different networks, most of which we have covered earlier in this chapter. Like many of its counterparts, it is used to track conversations and measure campaign results via the Internet and mobile devices.

Hootsuite has advanced functionality.

What is tracking?

Tracking is important because you can see which conversations are trending and where your messages are going; therefore, if your campaign is not successful you can make some changes.

Hootsuite has been largely free in the past, but now most of its functionality is charged for. It listens to your posts, and tracks feedback and comments. It is fabulous in some ways because its enterprise solution can manage unlimited social media profiles, it has enhanced analytics, an advanced campaign scheduling tool, and many other useful features. It is a complete solution; the product has advanced functionality but may be a little expensive for a start-up which does not specialise in social media.

Alternatives to Hootsuite

Let us look at the pros and cons of some of the alternatives to Hootsuite:

- **Buffer** – essentially a scheduling tool which allows you to plan when, during the day, you should post to social media. It does not 'listen' to your social media as does Hootsuite. You could use Hootsuite to listen, and Buffer to schedule your posts.

- **IFTTT** – the advantage of this tool is that it allows you to connect to major networks and channels to automate sharing on social media sites. So, you may have a Twitter account for example, you have set it up but every time you tweet it automatically appears on your Instagram page too. This is true for more than 365 different types of channels. You can set it up so that the automated posting contains any specified comments from yourself; these are called personal recipes.

- **SocialOomph** – this tool has plenty of functionality in both free and paid for varieties. There are functions for Facebook, Twitter, LinkedIn and others. For example, you can track keywords in Twitter, as well as mentions and reTweets.

- **Tweetdeck** – is a powerful solution which mainly focuses on Twitter. It now belongs to Twitter and you can schedule Tweets. Stay up-to-date with many other useful functions. Also look at **Tweepi.**

- **SocialFlow** – with this tool you can watch real-time conversations in social media; it is a live social media tool. Some big names including the Washington Post, use the services of SocialFlow. It catches the peak times for attention from particular target audiences; therefore, if you have a large audience, you can maximize when to post your Tweets. If you are spending money on advertising, SocialFlow also gives you a time-span on which to focus.

Conclusion

There are many more social media management tools out there. It is an expanding industry and new products and services come along all the time. Make sure that you are not buying into too much, and that anything that you purchase fits your budget and is clear and straightforward to use.

Your social media plan. What works best for you and your customers?

Social media	Objective 1	Objective 2	Objective 3
Content marketing			
Facebook			
Twitter			
LinkedIn			
Google +			
YouTube			
Instagram			
Pinterest			
Social media tools e.g. Hootsuite			

Chapter 15 Your e-mail marketing

For your start-up or small business, it is likely that your customers will like to hear from you again. E-mail marketing is an ideal medium for you to stay in regular touch with your customers. As with much digital marketing for small businesses, you can make this as simple or complex as you like. As you begin, ask yourself *what is it like to receive emails from my suppliers?* If you get too many e-mails you are likely to lose interest, and you might unsubscribe. If you Do not get enough emails, you will could think that the supplier has forgotten about you. The most important thing is to keep your list current and fresh. Let us have a look at how you could undertake your e-mail marketing campaign. We will also consider suitable providers of the marketing services to your start up or small business.

Your email marketing campaign

Let us take a look at the best way for you to design your e-mail marketing campaign. As with most other types of marketing, e-mail marketing campaigns work best if they are planned beforehand.

Email marketing still has opportunities

Based on marketing principles ask yourself who exactly are you targeting your e-mail at? Who are your customers and clients? Who is your target audience? There may be a number of segments that you are targeting, and in which case you would adapt or change your e-mail campaign. This is quite important, because different segments will require different marketing messages.

Let us return to our budget piano. One e-mail marketing message might be for teenagers, and another might be for retired piano players. The teenagers will be attracted to the cheap piano because they want to try out a new instrument without committing themselves to too high a price. The retired players may already have piano playing skills, but they need to replace an aging or broken piano; they too are on a low budget. You would need to tailor the message for each potential customer. Your copy and content will need to reflect this.

Keep the message short and clear

Keep the message short and clear, and use constant and straightforward text. Your logo needs to be strongly placed at the top of the e-mail, and the first few sentences are your opportunity to make an impact, because if they do not, the recipient will not read on. Copywriting and content writing skills are important for e-mail marketing. Nevertheless, try to keep the message clear and brief. Keep it focused upon your target group.

Funnel to website or social media

Once the recipient has opened your e-mail you need to direct them through a text or image link to your website, or social media. Hence you need a landing page on your site and/or a social media page that will take the recipient through to the next stage.

Funnel recipients to your digital pages

This is also known as 'funnelling,' where the funnelling starts wide and then directs the recipient to the point of purchase. Your landing page needs to be consistent with your brand and also the e-mail. Key aspects of your offering need to be repeated on the landing page to reassure your recipient, and again include a **Call-To-Action (CTA)** to move them towards the final stage of purchase or signup (obviously, this depends on what your purpose is).

Test your email

Next you need to test your e-mail. This is really simple when you use one of the popular e-mail marketing services. Simply send an e-mail to yourself or to staff and colleagues, and ask them to respond with any necessary changes. This is also reassuring for you. Testing is vital, so Do not cut corners here. You will almost always make changes.

Measure your results

The campaign must be measured and monitored, so that you can compare and contrast the success of various strategies. You can measure all sorts of indicators including how many e-mails were delivered, and how many were opened, how many recipients clicked on your link and began their journey through your funnel. You should be able to compare the amount of e-mails which you sent to your actual sales. Again, some e-mail marketing providers allow you to measure the value of each individual client in your mailing list, and you can rank and prioritise them.

Keep your mailing list updated

This also allows you to remove individuals from your mailing list who Do not open your e-mails and will never become customers. Again, this may reduce the cost of the mailing. The mailing list needs to be current – so if many of your emails bounce, remain unopened or induce the client to unsubscribe, then you need to refresh your list and/or change your approach. Always keep your list fresh and up to date, it is an evolving business tool.

Keep trying new ideas. By comparing and contrasting your relative success you will make your campaigns more effective. By changing small details, you may notice unexpected improvements.

You need to set yourself SMART objectives for your mailings. For example, *to inform my 100, 000 strong mailing list about a product range launch within seven days*. You also would need to consider the finance needed to plan, write, implement and monitor the online campaign. Measuring your campaign is vital, and all e-mail marketing service providers give you a toolkit to control your plan, and there is always Google Analytics in addition. Other sections of this book will consider Google analytics in more detail.

Segment Target Position (STP)

Having decided that you are going to prepare your campaign you will need to segment, target, and position your message not only for the entire email-shot, but also for each individual that you are communicating with. Your campaign should have meaning for everyone with whom you are in contact. Your purpose is to achieve a sale or Call-To-Action, and success is more often down to realistic segmentation rather than creativity. Segment Target Position (STP) is covered in more detail in earlier sections.

Distinguish your title

To grab the attention of your reader you need to make sure that your subject line or title, jumps out and distinguishes itself from the other communications in your potential customer's inbox. This will also help you overcome spam filters. Keep it relevant to your topic and include your website name where possible, for example *French Teacher Launches New Course*, which would be of interest to your clients.

Create great emails!

Next – you need to get creative! As with all marketing communications it is important that you design an email structure or template which is strong enough to entice and retain customers. So here are a few tips to help you to construct engaging e-mails.

- Remember to give your respondents the opportunity to **unsubscribe** from your mailing list. It may be that respondents have changed jobs or have other interests and no longer require your services.

- Keep the actual physical size of the **e-mail small** enough for your client's e-mail program or browser to be able to open it. If you pack it with Flash imagery many e-mail packages will not open anyway, and think about those people in countries where bandwidth is narrow, and where the Internet service will be much slower.

- Therefore, it is also good advice to give readers the **choice of HTML or text** versions of your correspondence.

- Write in **simple language** so that readers can quickly scan through your message.

- The **Call-To-Action (CTA)** should be prominent. This is what you want the respondent to do as a result of reading your message. As with many of the other tools which are used for small business digital marketing, you will learn as you experience more campaigns. Make sure you keep notes, and as time goes on your online e-mail campaigns will become more and more effective.

It might be best to use e-mail marketing as part of a more integrated campaign, so that solely relying upon e-mail does not leave you exposed. For example, remind your clients that you're about to have a sale, or include some taster or teaser information for a new product launch.

E-mail marketing providers

There are many companies out there that will automate your e-mail marketing for you, and it is recommended that this is what you should do. In fact, many of them will do your automation for free until you hit the specific threshold of signups of around 2000 e-mail addresses. Such companies would include Mailchimp, Constant Contact, iContact and many, many others.

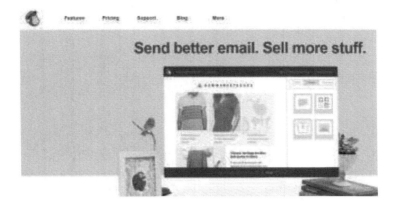

The bigger providers offer keen deals, with plenty of flexibility.

Set up stages

1. You would start by registering online, and setting up payment details with your credit card.

2. Make sure that your website and social media have places to 'sign up' for emails. This will help you build a free database of potential customers based upon past visitor or customers. Please remember to make it easy to unsubscribe. Email providers will make setting up sign up pages simple to install. Too much? Then ask your email provider or website developer for help.

3. You can alter the information that you want to collect such as e-mail addresses, names and locations. However, do not make your customers' initial sign -up too onerous because you Do not want to scare potential customers away by asking them to do too much.

4. The customer will then receive an e-mail which allows them to *opt-in*, generally by clicking on a simple link. It must also be simple for your recipient to *unsubscribe* or *change* their details as and when necessary. In fact, this is the law in many parts of the world.

5. You must also include a business or personal address to make your e-mails trustworthy and to reassure your signups that you are who you say you are. This will reassure your recipients that you are a reliable and trustworthy small business.

There are plenty of e-mail marketing companies out there. One thing is sure, that when your business grows, you need to make your e-mail marketing solution as automatic as possible, so Do not think that you can manually enter details on your tablet or PC.

E-mail marketing providers give you plenty of interactive functionality today. They will build lists for you, they will give you custom or bespoke e-mail forms and newsletters, you could integrate your mailing list with Facebook and other social media providers, and there are other features which will sync the mailing list with other customer databases or shopping carts, for example. You are often offered multiple databases and lists within a single e-mail marketing package and companies will bill you monthly or by the amount of mail you send e.g. $30 monthly or for 10,000 e-mails. Shop around for the best prices, and read reviews from other small businesses. As your business grows, your e-mail marketing list will grow. So, expect to pay approximately $30.00 per month for unlimited emails to 3000 recipients. This is an incentive to keep your mailing list clear and up to date.

Try not to send too many e-mails to your clients. One or possibly two emails per month will be enough. Any more than that will be considered spam, and will reduce the interest that your clients have in your emails.

Conclusion

Email marketing is far from obsolete. You will need to keep a detailed and comprehensive list of email addresses as clients become loyal, and as you get new ones. It is the starting point of Customer Relationship Management (CRM) which is not only about recruiting new customers, but also keeping them and marketing future goods, services and ideas to them.

Chapter 16 Measuring your online success

Google Analytics

You would be forgiven for being confused about Google Analytics. It is often discussed in business circles and amongst the web design community, as if it is something which is entirely taken for granted. **Google analytics is simply a free web site analysis service.**

Google Analytics is a free and powerful tool

It gives you data about your website. It has a lot of functionality, probably far more than any small business will ever need. However, the key to using Google analytics successfully is to select only those features that will be useful to you. Do not overburden yourself with over complex website analytics if you do not make money on it. On the other hand, if your site and social media are fundamental to your business and you anticipate plenty of traffic, then Google Analytics might unlock success! Brilliant! Let us have a look at Google analytics in more detail.

What is Google analytics?

Google analytics is a free web site analysis service provided by Google, which tracks and reports on web traffic. It is by far the most widely adopted website analytics service on the web. In addition to being free, or freemium, there are also paid-for versions namely Google analytics 360 which is targeted at businesses, and Google Analytics for Mobile Apps which is aimed at analysing data from iOS (Apple devices such iPhones) and Android apps, such as the Samsung Galaxy range of Smartphones.

Get started with Google Analytics

1. Sign up for your free Google Analytics account.
   https://analytics.google.com

2. In your new account, set up your first website or *property*. This is your website, but you can add others in the future if you wish.

3. Set up web tracking. This means cut and paste code supplied to you by Google during this sign-up process. Paste it into your websites pages, generally into the header. If you are using WordPress, download a simple plugin to do this for you. You could even use a *header* plugin, and cut and paste the code there.

4. Bookmark the dashboard. All done! Obviously, you need to leave it for a few days or weeks so that it can track your data.

You view your Google Analytics data using this clear dashboard.

So, what features will be useful to your small business? Let us take a look at a few.

- If you decided to go with **Google AdWords**, now you can get some very precise data about the people that are looking at your adverts. You can review your online campaign by tracking the quality of the landing page (i.e. when the advert is clicked, this is the page on your website where the person clicking is taken – it could be a product, for example).

- If you have set yourself some **goals for conversion**, you can measure them. Your goals might include how many file downloads you have had, any pages that have been viewed, how many newsletter signups you have had, how many people have telephoned you directly, or how many products or services you have sold.

- You can look at your **successful pages**, as well as those that performed poorly, and you can do comparisons. It shows you where customers have come from, for example United States, and which state the visitors have come from. It tells you how long they stayed on your site, which pages they entered via, and left through.

Country	Sessions	% New Sessions	New Users	Bounce Rate	Pages/Session	Avg. Session Duration	Goal Conversion Rate
	181,159	79.63%	144,260	85.41%	1.32	00:01:13	0.00%
1. United States	66,305	82.65%	56,452	90.13%	1.18	00:00:46	0.00%
2. United Kingdom	15,653	79.03%	12,370	82.00%	1.46	00:01:30	0.00%
3. India	12,410	78.20%	9,704	82.36%	1.30	00:01:31	0.00%
4. Malaysia	6,820	71.06%	4,846	84.12%	1.31	00:01:30	0.00%
5. Philippines	6,623	87.30%	5,782	82.03%	1.30	00:01:34	0.00%
6. Australia	6,308	75.09%	4,774	82.48%	1.41	00:01:24	0.00%
7. Brazil	5,790	90.42%	5,226	87.95%	1.23	00:00:58	0.00%
8. Canada	4,425	84.66%	3,748	91.14%	1.20	00:00:37	0.00%
9. Kenya	3,297	71.97%	2,373	79.07%	1.44	00:01:46	0.00%
10. Singapore	2,464	69.37%	1,701	90.05%	1.30	00:01:02	0.00%

You can see the geographical location of your visitors

- Again, if you are trading online and expecting lots of traffic, there are features including **advanced segmentation.**

- If you have an **ecommerce website**, you can get reports which tracks sales activity and performance. Basic ecommerce information is given such as revenue, the number of transactions, and many other online commerce related metrics.

- The idea is that you only set up the services which are necessary, otherwise you're wasting valuable time which could be better spent elsewhere promoting your small business.

- A unique feature of Google analytics is called **Real Time analytics**. This shows you in real time how many visitors you have on your website, and what they're looking at. This is real Big Brother!

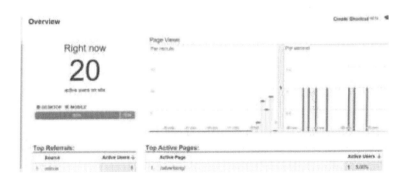

See in 'real time' your website's active users.

- You have the opportunity to set up **100 website profiles**, which for most small businesses will be far too many. However, if you do intend to have a number of websites trading online, you can keep them in one place using a single user profile.
- If you are setting up **mobile apps**, you need to go through the same process to set up for the first time. If you are already a Google analytics user, you need to go to your account. Select

admin and then in the *property* column, create a *new property* from the drop-down menu. Simply select *mobile app.*

- If you want to learn more, Google has a free Google Analytics Academy. https://analyticsacademy.withgoogle.com/. It is free and you can go directly to what you need to know. If in doubt, recruit the services of your website developer.

What are your needs? Learn from the Google Analytics Academy.

Google Webmaster Tools – Your Search Console.

One of the most vital tools for Google success is Your Search Console. Google search console is a free service that helps you monitor the *general performance* of your website in the Google search engine rankings. Let us be clear about this, for your website to be included within Google's search rankings, you Do not need to sign-up to the service! However, it gives you a clear summary of how well your site is performing, and as you make changes and develop your website. It gives you an indication of how successful you are.

Google's webmaster tools give an overview of your site's performance.

Google's clear and succinct dashboard is straightforward to use. This is why Google's webmaster tools are also useful to you and your start-up. Here are the main uses.

- **Messages from Google** about your website's status in their search engine. Whilst these messages are largely automatically generated, they are really useful because Google communicates with you directly about your website and how it is set up in the search engine. For example, if your website goes down for any period of time Google will detect this and send you a message.

- **Search appearance** gives an overview of how your website appears in the search engine. This is the technical data. The most useful section here relates to HTML improvements, where any issues with your meta description, title tags and non-indexable content are flagged. For example, some pages may have no meta descriptions. You can add better descriptions which make your website more appealing to the search engine. There are other more technical free services too – such as the data highlighter. Take a look at these and if they do not seem useful Do not use them!

- **Search Traffic** is a far more useful feature.

- The software gives you really interesting information in relation to which *search terms* people are using in the search engines to get to your website. So, searching for *grand piano, cheap piano, cheap piano Boston*? Therefore, you can see what the most popular or trending search terms are.

- You have a summary of all of the *links to your website*. Links are important because Google uses them as positive votes for your content; so, the more votes you get to a particular page the better chance it has of ranking higher in the search engine. Conversely, if there are some spam links to your website, from less reputable sources, this may negatively affect your website's appearance in the search engine.

- The tool gives an overview of your *internal links*. This is important mainly so that visitors can easily navigate your website, and get to the content they want quickly. This also has a positive bearing on your website's performance in Google's search engine.

- You can set the *international target* to your own country. So, if you are trading in the United States, set the international target to the USA. For example, if your site is written in Spanish, you can change the *language* settings in this section as well. You will also be able to check the mobile usability of your website.

- **Google index** tells you how many pages of your website have been added to Google's search engine. You will also be able to disclose which keyword is most popular in relation to your website, for example piano. This means that some keywords are being searched for far more than others, and this will help you to write new content.

- **Crawl** allows you to find out if there are any errors in your site. This is useful if the search engine struggles to access certain parts of your content. You simply put it right, and then check back again to make sure that any issues have been alleviated.

  - It will also tell you about the activity of the Googlebot in relation to your website over the last 90 days. Remember Googlebot is the piece of software which Google uses to audit your website in relation to how it performs in their search engine.

  - You can also find out how long it takes for your visitors to download pages; the faster, the better!

  - A surprisingly useful free feature is *Fetch as Google*. If you have had trouble with your website, perhaps it has been down for a short period time, then you can instigate the Googlebot by using this feature.

  - You get feedback on your **sitemap**, and a summary of any errors with pages. It is a really good idea to check your sitemap at regular intervals, perhaps every couple of months, but especially if you have made large changes to the site - its content or structure. If you do not have a sitemap, you really need to add one. If you use WordPress, add any popular plugin and activate it.

- **Security** issues detect whether your website has been hacked. If you are unfortunate enough for this to happen, Google will detect it and direct you to resources to solve the problem.

- **Other resources** are available from Google to help you improve your website. Once you register with webmaster tools, browse some of these resources to see if any of them suit you and your small business.

Conclusions

Sign up for the FREE Google tools such as Analytics and Webmaster Tools, and start measuring your success. As you get more information about the success and failures of your digital activities, you will be able to change and fine-tune your digital marketing approaches. Over time you will become more knowledgeable about maximising your online presence.

Chapter 17 International marketing for growing businesses

Are there any marketing opportunities in other countries?

International marketing is likely to be a medium to long-term strategy for most entrepreneurs, start-ups and small businesses. However, by trading overseas there is an opportunity for marketing that you may realise more quickly than you think. There are a couple of key marketing issues that you need to deal with; firstly, you have to ask yourself, how am I going to actually get into a foreign market? Secondly, you need to work out which approach is best to actually get into the market. Both of these key questions are answered in the following sections, and as with the rest of this book, you need to adapt these approaches, or processes, to your own business situation.

Your idea, product or service has a global market

How to Enter a Foreign Market

The **International Marketing Entry Evaluation Process** is a five-stage process, and its purpose is to gauge which international market or markets offer the best opportunities for our products or services to succeed. The five steps are *Country Identification, Preliminary Screening, In-Depth Screening, Final Selection* and *Direct Experience*. Let us take a look at each step in turn.

Step One - Country Identification

The World is your oyster. You can choose any country to go into. So, you conduct country identification - which means that you undertake a general overview of potential new markets. There might be a simple match - for example two countries might share a similar heritage e.g. the United Kingdom and Australia, a similar language e.g. the United States and Australia, or even a similar culture, political ideology or religion e.g. China and Cuba. Often selection at this stage is more straightforward, for example, a country might be nearby e.g. Canada and the United States. Alternatively, your export market is in the same trading zone e.g. the European Union. Again, at this point it is very early days and potential export markets could be included or discarded for any number of reasons.

Step Two - Preliminary Screening

At this second stage, one takes a more serious look at those countries remaining after undergoing preliminary screening. Now you begin to score, weight and rank nations based upon macro-economic factors such as currency stability, exchange rates, level of domestic consumption and so on. Now you have the basis to start calculating the nature of market entry costs. Some countries such as China require that some fraction of the company entering the market is owned domestically - this would need to be considered. There are some nations that are experiencing political instability and any company entering such a market would need to be rewarded for the risk that they would take. At this point you could decide upon a shorter list of countries that you would wish to enter. Now in-depth screening can begin.

Step Three - In-Depth Screening

The countries that make it to stage three would all be considered feasible for market entry. So, it is vital that detailed information on the target market is obtained so that marketing decision-making can be accurate. Now one can deal with not only micro-economic factors but also local conditions such as marketing research in relation to the marketing mix i.e. what prices can be charged in the nation? - How does one distribute a product or service such as ours in the nation? How should we communicate with our target segments in the nation? How does our product or service need to be adapted for the nation? All of this information will form the basis of segmentation, targeting and positioning. One could also take into account the value of the nation's market, any tariffs or quotas in operation, and similar opportunities or threats to new entrants.

Step Four - Final Selection

Now a final short-list of potential nations is decided upon. You would reflect upon strategic goals and look for a match in the nations at hand. The company could look at close competitors or similar domestic companies that have already entered the market to get firmer costs in relation to market entry. You could also look at other nations that your business has already entered to see if there are any similarities, or learning that can be used to assist with decision-making in this instance. A final scoring, ranking and weighting can be undertaken based upon more focused criteria. After this exercise the marketing manager should probably try to visit the final handful of nations remaining on the short, short-list.

Step Five - Direct Experience

Personal experience is important. You or your representatives should travel to a particular nation to experience first-hand the nation's culture and business practices. On a first impressions basis, at least one can ascertain in what ways the nation is similar or dissimilar to your own domestic market or the others in which your company already trades. Now you will need to be careful in respect of self-referencing. Remember that your experience to date is based upon your life mainly in your own nation and your expectations will be based upon what your already know. Try to be flexible and experimental in new nations, and Do not be judgemental - it is about what's best for your company - happy hunting.

Getting into an international market – who to deal with.

Once you've decided which nation or nations that you are going to trade with, the next job is to work out how best to get into the market. You need to know who to deal with in each nation. The next section looks at what we call modes of entry. A mode of entry is simply the way of trading with a partner in a different country, for example using an agent.

Modes of entry into an international market are the channels which your organisation employs to gain entry to a new international market. This section considers a number of key choices, but recognizes that alternatives are many and diverse. Here you will be considering modes of entry into international markets such as *the Internet, Exporting, Licensing, International Agents, International Distributors, Strategic Alliances, Joint Ventures, Overseas Manufacture and International Sales Subsidiaries.* Finally, we consider the Stages of Internationalization.

Licensing

Licensing includes **franchising, turnkey contracts and contract manufacturing.**

- *Licensing* is where your own organization charges a fee and/or royalty for the use of its technology, brand and/or expertise.
- *Franchising* involves the organization (franchiser) providing branding, concepts, expertise, and in fact most facets that are needed to operate in an overseas market, to the franchisee. Management tends to be controlled by the franchiser. Examples include Domino's Pizza, Coffee Republic and McDonald's Restaurants.
- *Turnkey contracts* are major strategies to build large plants. They often include the training and development of key employees where skills are sparse – for example, Toyota's car plant in Adapazari, Turkey. You would not own the plant once it is handed over.

International Agents and International Distributors

Agents are often an early step into international marketing. Put simply, agents are individuals or organizations that are contracted to your business, and market on your behalf in a particular country. They rarely take ownership of products, and more commonly take a commission on goods sold. Agents usually represent more than one organization. Agents are a low-cost, but low-control option. If you intend to globalize, make sure that your contract allows you to regain direct control of your product, service or idea. Of course, you need to set targets since you never know the level of commitment of your agent. Agents might also represent your competitors – so beware conflicts of interest. They tend to be expensive to recruit, retain and train. *Distributors* are similar to agents, with the main difference that distributors take ownership of the goods. Therefore, they have an incentive to market products and to make a profit from them. Otherwise pros and cons are similar to those of international agents.

Strategic Alliances (SA)

Strategic alliances is a term that describes a whole series of different relationships between companies that market internationally. Sometimes the relationships are between competitors. There are many examples including:

- Shared manufacturing.
- Research and Development (R&D) arrangements.
- Distribution alliances.
- Marketing agreements.

Essentially, Strategic Alliances are non-equity based agreements i.e. companies remain independent and separate.

Joint Ventures (JV) and Modes of Entry

Joint Ventures tend to be equity-based i.e. a new company is set up with parties owning a proportion of the new business. There are many reasons why companies set up Joint Ventures to assist them to enter a new international market:

- Access to technology, core competences or management skills.
- To gain entry to a foreign market. For example, any business wishing to enter China needs to source local Chinese partners.
- Access to distribution channels, manufacturing and R&D are most common forms of Joint Venture.

Overseas Manufacture or International Sales Subsidiary

A business may decide that none of the other options are as viable as actually owning an *overseas manufacturing plant* i.e. the organization invests in plant, machinery and labour in the overseas market. This is also known as Foreign Direct Investment (FDI). This can be a new-build, or the company might acquire a current business that has suitable plant. Of course, you could assemble products in the new plant, and simply export components from the home market (or another country). The key benefit is that your business becomes localized – you manufacture for customers in the market in which you are trading. You also will gain local market knowledge and be able to adapt products and services to the needs of local consumers. The downside is that you take on the risk associated with the local domestic market. An International *Sales Subsidiary* would be similar, reducing the element of risk, and have the same key benefit of course. However, it acts more like a distributor that is owned by your own company.

Internationalization Stages, and modes of entry

So, having considered the key modes of entry into international markets, we conclude by considering the Stages of Internationalization. Some companies will never trade overseas and so do not go through a single stage. Others will start at a later or even the last stage. Of course, some will go through each stage as summarized now:

- Indirect exporting or licensing
- Direct exporting via a local distributor
- Your own foreign presence
- Home manufacture, and foreign assembly
- Foreign manufacture

It is worth noting that not all authorities on international marketing agree as to which mode of entry sits where. For example, some see *franchising* as a standalone mode, whilst others see *franchising as part of licensing*. In reality, the most important point is that you consider all useful modes of entry into international markets – over and above which pigeon-hole it fits into.

The Internet

The Internet is a new channel for some organizations and the sole channel for a large number of innovative new organizations. The digital marketing space consists of new Internet companies that have emerged as the Internet has developed, as well as those pre-existing companies that now employ digital marketing approaches as part of their overall marketing plan. For some companies, the Internet is an additional channel that enhances or replaces their traditional channel(s). For others, the Internet has provided the opportunity for a new online company.

Refer to sections of this book which considers digital and social media marketing. By using Amazon, eBay, or similar channels, you will achieve some form of International Marketing with relative ease.

Exporting

There are **direct** and **indirect** approaches to exporting to other nations. Direct exporting is straightforward. Essentially the organization makes a commitment to market overseas on its own behalf. This gives it greater control over its brand and operations overseas, over and above indirect exporting. On the other hand, if you were to employ a home country agency (i.e. an exporting company from your country – which handles exporting on your behalf) to get your product into an overseas market then you would be exporting indirectly. Examples of indirect exporting include:

- *Piggybacking* whereby your new product uses the existing distribution and logistics of another business.
- *Export Management Houses (EMHs)* that act as a bolt on export department for your company. They offer a whole

range of bespoke or a la carte services to exporting
organizations.

- *Consortia* are groups of small or medium-sized organizations
that group together to market related, or sometimes unrelated
products in international markets.
- *Trading companies* were started when some nations decided
that they wished to have overseas colonies. They date back to
an imperialist past that some nations might prefer to forget
e.g. the British, French, Spanish and Portuguese colonies.
Today they exist as mainstream businesses that use traditional
business relationships as part of their competitive advantage.

Again, it may be that some of these alternatives are a long way off for
your business. However, if you work in a very fine or segmented
markets, or industrial markets, it is possible that some of these
alternatives may be useful to you quite quickly. International
Marketing is a really good way to grow your business, so try be
familiar with opportunities to seize them once they arise.

The last few sections focus upon International Marketing, or consider
key issues for any small business entering a foreign market. Pricing for
international markets is always a popular topic. The next section
summarises your choices in relation to pricing, as well as the factors to
take into account when you are setting price.

International Pricing Approaches

- **Export Pricing** – a price is set for by the home-based marketing
managers for the international market. The pricing approach is
based upon a whole series of factors which are driven by the
influences on pricing listed above. Then mainstream
approaches to pricing may be implemented – see below.
- **Non-cash payments** – less and less popular these days, non-
cash payments include counter-trade where goods are
exchanged for goods between companies from different parts
of the world.
- **Transfer Pricing** – prices are set in the home market, and goods
are effectively sold to the international subsidiary which then
attaches its own margin based upon the best price that local